Live Well, Teach Well

OTHER TITLES FROM BLOOMSBURY EDUCATION

How to Survive in Teaching: Without imploding, exploding or walking away, by Dr Emma Kell

Wellbeing in the Primary Classroom: A practical guide to teaching happiness, by Adrian Bethune

Mental Health Matters, by Paula Nagel

Teaching Happiness and Well-Being in Schools, by Ian Morris

Teach, Reflect, Doodle, by Paul Wright

100 Ideas for Primary Teachers: Mindfulness in the Classroom, by Tammie Prince

Live Well, Teach Well

A practical approach to wellbeing that works

Abigail Mann

BLOOMSBURY EDUCATION
LONDON OXFORD NEW YORK NEW DELHI SYDNEY

BLOOMSBURY EDUCATION
Bloomsbury Publishing Plc
50 Bedford Square, London, WC1B 3DP, UK

BLOOMSBURY, BLOOMSBURY EDUCATION and the Diana logo are trademarks of
Bloomsbury Publishing Plc

First published in Great Britain 2018

A catalogue record for this book is available from the British Library.

ISBN: PB: 978-1-4729-4979-0; ePDF: 978-1-4729-4977-6; ePub: 978-1-4729-4976-9

2 4 6 8 10 9 7 5 3 1 (paperback)

Typeset by Newgen KnowledgeWorks Pvt. Ltd., Chennai, India
Printed and bound in the UK by CPI Group (UK) Ltd, Croydon CR0 4YY

All papers used by Bloomsbury Publishing Plc are natural, recyclable products from
wood grown in well-managed forests. The manufacturing processes conform to the
environmental regulations of the country of origin.

To find out more about our authors and books visit www.bloomsbury.com
and sign up for our newsletters.

Contents

Chapter 3: Working smarter 37

Chapter 4: Rocking teaching and learning 59

Chapter 5: Supporting pupils 79

Acknowledgements

To all the colleagues who have supported me throughout my teaching career, I dedicate this book to you. Staff of Long Field Academy, Barnwell School, Whitefield School and Twitter colleagues, without your care and support, ideas like this book are not possible. I am lucky to be surrounded by such supportive colleagues.

To the students I have taught over the years and the students I teach now, I dedicate this book to you. It's because of you I believe I have the best job in the world.

To all the contributors, thank you, thank you, thank you. Without your ideas, this book would not be what it is. I dedicate this book to you.

To the teaching and learnings ladies, Rebeka, Rebecca, Jackie and Naomi. Thank you for being my cheerleaders and for keeping me sane! I dedicate this book to you.

To Rhea and Rachel, for being there then and for being here now. I dedicate this book to you.

To my father, who taught me never to give up and to 'run like the wind' in all my endeavours, I dedicate this book to you.

To my mother, who taught me the most important thing of all: to be kind. I dedicate this book to you.

'Hope rises like a phoenix from the ashes of shattered dreams.' S. A. Sachs

Introduction

Teacher wellbeing has become something of a hot topic over the past few years. To understand why this is the case, you only have to ask a teacher how they are feeling mid-term during any term throughout the year. Across the country, many teachers are experiencing high levels of pressure, stress and exhaustion. Since I began teaching in 2010, the problem does not seem to have improved. In some cases, teaching colleagues have left the profession altogether. Between 2010 and 2015, 10,000 teachers left the profession and the numbers are rising. Increasing working hours and unmanageable workloads are responsible for the current situation.

Whilst the government attempts to tackle the problem at a national level, responsible headteachers across the nation are desperately trying to improve workload issues for their staff. In addition, teachers are doing what they can to redress their work/life balance and improve their wellbeing.

The idea for this book came about at a time when I had decided to focus on my own wellbeing. Working over 60 hours per week was affecting my wellbeing and I was dealing with some personal challenges too. I needed to refocus on what was important, so I began sharing ideas on Twitter and used a blog-sharing platform called Staffrm to write about wellbeing ideas and how to gain back some of your social time. A friend suggested I share the ideas through a book proposal, and Bloomsbury were good enough to accept it.

The book is split into seven chapters, all designed to promote teacher wellbeing. In each of them, you will find practical ideas to support either yourself or those around you. The chapters cover: looking after your own wellbeing; recognising the wellbeing of those with whom you work; improving teaching and learning to ensure your own wellbeing is maintained; supporting pupils and their wellbeing; strengthening community links to support your own wellbeing; and whole-school wellbeing.

I suggest you use the book as a 'pick-up-and-look' resource for when you need it most. For example, if you are struggling to manage your time, the chapter titled 'Working smarter' can help you. If you are look-ing to develop wellbeing on a larger scale, the chapters titled 'Whole-school wellbeing' or 'Community care' can support you with this.

When I think about it, it seems utterly ridiculous that a book like mine should even exist in the teaching world, but until such time as things are much improved, I hope you find it useful.

Chapter 1

Wiser wellbeing

How to look after your own wellbeing.

At the risk of sounding terribly condescending, we all need to remember to look after ourselves from time to time. This is something I need to remind myself of a fair few times throughout the year too. Teachers work hard, sometimes far too hard for their own good. Let's be honest, at the heart of teaching is the goodwill of committed teachers every-where. At certain points in the year, teaching seems almost too difficult, and it is at these times that teacher burnout can happen. Unless you actively aim to focus on your wellbeing, burnout might be unavoidable.

This chapter is all about looking after yourself so that you can get on and do the job you love. There are ideas about how to survive certain pressure points throughout the year, how to create a teacher survival kit and how to take some well-deserved time out during the middle of the week. The key here is to make sure you actually have some downtime. I know this is difficult when you have so much to do, believe me, but you are no good to anyone if you aren't at your best and energised for the task at hand. I hope you will find some useful ideas in this chapter and I would love to hear all about how you are taking back control of your wellbeing. Use the hashtags at the end of each idea to let me know on Twitter.

Idea 1: Build a network

Working as a team will improve your teaching and save you time.

As a teacher, there will be times during the year when you may need to look outside your school and seek knowledge and advice from an extended network of professionals. This will have a positive impact on wellbeing, as it will help you to grow more confident in your role and feel better supported. Below are just some of the ways in which you can build connections and therefore improve your wellbeing.

Visit local schools
Visit other schools in your area. Whatever you teach, it's always a great idea to build strong connections with your neighbouring schools. Arrange an informal visit to see how other schools are doing things.

Meet regularly with other schools
Better still, set up regular meetings with other schools to share ideas and resources. I meet with other heads of English in this way every half term and it's proven valuable to work together on many different curriculum areas. This idea could work for any teacher, whether they are primary- or secondary-based. Find out what's out there and if there is no event relevant to you already, set your own up and start networking.

Join Twitter
Join Twitter and start connecting with like-minded professionals. I joined Twitter in 2009 but didn't really begin to use it until 2014. I can honestly say it is one of the best things I have ever done in terms of my professional development. I have become a far better teacher since joining, not least because of the huge amount of advice and support available.

Attend TeachMeets
Attend TeachMeets that are taking place in your area. These free events are filled with teachers sharing everyday ideas that work in their classroom. Over the course of the evening, educators will present in two- or seven-minute slots. I always tell anyone who attends to take at least one idea home with them to try in their classroom the following week.

#buildanetwork
#connect

Idea 2: Preparation perfect

The key to consistent focus on your wellbeing is good preparation.

Deciding to make a change to your wellbeing is one thing, but putting it into practice can seem like a difficult process when you are in the thick of a new school term. Suddenly, all of those well-intentioned ideas seem to dissipate under the stress of having a thousand things to do before the upcoming week. However, there is a way around this. Plan. Plan. Plan.

Here are some of the changes you can make to ensure a smooth working week that also allows for more downtime:

* Check the school calendar regularly to prepare for any particularly busy weeks. Knowing the pressure points in the year allows you to plan more effectively. You may decide not to go out in the evening that week and choose to have a night in to relax instead.
* Plan for the week ahead on Friday or even earlier. If you leave it until the weekend, you are risking overworking and not getting the much-needed break that the weekends provide.
* Have a cut-off time for work in the evenings and stick to it. No excuses.
* Plan to exercise three times a week if you can. A 30-minute session is all it takes to keep you feeling fresh and energised throughout the week.
* Avoid leaving your laundry until the weekend. Do it in the week to prevent a last-minute rush on Sunday evening.
* Prepare your weekly meals in advance. This saves time, as you no longer need to prepare meals in the evenings, and ensures you stay healthy; you can prepare fresh meals full of goodness and avoid less healthy options in the school canteen. Finally, it saves a fair amount of money each week, as you are less likely to buy food on the go.

Of course, all these ideas take time and habitual practice to put in place, but if you take them one idea at a time, over the course of the year, you will begin to see a real difference in your wellbeing.

#perfectprep
#exercise
#notice

Idea 3: Exam season survival

Planning ahead for exam season will keep you feeling cool and calm throughout the process.

When exam season takes hold, it can be one of the most tiring times of the academic year. Your wellbeing is naturally affected as working hours increase. Pupils suddenly want all the help you can offer, past papers are instantly pouring off your desk, meetings seem to double and data tracking becomes intense and frequent (even though it really shouldn't). Before exam season even gets close, consider the tips below to make it more efficient and manageable. This will ensure your wellbeing is not impacted too much.

- Know the exam dates well in advance and make sure pupils do too. This will keep you focused on the end goal.
- Prepare your resources before exam season arrives. Create folders of mock papers and mark schemes and have resources readily available in your classroom for pupils to take whenever they wish. This saves so much time, as usually pupils will be at your door asking for extra work when you are least prepared.
- Keep one weekday evening free each week. Make sure you go home early and do nothing work-related when you get there. I do this every week now and the impact it has had on my wellbeing is notable. Make it mid-week to ensure the week is broken up into manageable sections.
- Create a revision timetable for pupils. This works wonders for me, as it's easy to follow and ensures every topic is given the same amount of revision time. Pupils love this too because they know exactly what they will be learning each day. Add an attendance and topic checklist at the end, so pupils will know which areas to revise if they miss a lesson. This saves you time trying to figure out what they missed. Share the exam revision timetable with parents too. The more supportive they are, the easier you will find the exam period, as they will work to keep their child focused as much as you do.
- Structure your individual revision lessons. It can be all too easy to allow pupils to revise independently, but in my experience, this has only ever resulted in poor learning and wasted time. Avoid this like the plague! Keep your lessons structured and direct the pupils with

their revision. This will ensure that far more information is revised and retained.

- Interleave your revision lessons. Students learn more effectively if their topics are interleaved and spread out across the revision season rather than chunked. Ebbinghaus's 'forgetting curve' is a useful tool to help plan your revision timetable. Hermann Ebbinghaus was a German psychologist who studied how memory works. His forgetting curve shows how newly learned information can be forgotten over time if there is no attempt to retain it. It is useful as a planning aid because you can learn when to introduce topics to increase the chances of pupils retaining and remembering the information.

- Use high-challenge, low-threat revision strategies like quizzing and flashcards. These add an element of fun to the revision lesson whilst still developing pupil understanding. There are many online websites for these kinds of activities. Kahoot (www.kahoot.com) is great for quizzing and Plickers (www.plickers.com) is brilliant for those who have limited access to the internet for pupil use.

- Encourage pupils to mind map their topics. Mind maps are perfect visual aids for pupils and can help some pupils commit ideas to memory. Pupils can of course make these the old-fashioned way using paper, but there are now plenty of digital formats to choose from too. One example is GoConqr (www.goconqr.com), which combines a number of revision tools, such as mind maps, flashcards and quizzes, and other useful study tools.

- It's important to note that extra revision lessons are optional. You do not have to agree to do them. You should only agree if you are absolutely comfortable with it, and if you do agree, make sure you don't undertake too many. Extra lessons can have a significant impact on your time and wellbeing, which in turn affects pupil progress.

The key thing to remember is to plan ahead for busy times of the year, such as exam season. If you can pinpoint pressure points in the school year, you can plan to make them more manageable.

#examsurvival
#notice
#learn

Idea 4: Snack attack

You are what you eat, as they say. Eating the right foods will give you the energy to get through the day.

There will undoubtedly be times during the academic year where you are really struggling to get through the term. A balanced and healthy diet is obviously a necessity but, as we all know, this doesn't always go to plan. However, there are certain foods that will pick you up and provide that much-needed energy boost when you need it most. Eating healthily will ensure your wellbeing remains a focus throughout the year.

Here are my top snacks:

1. **Nuts** – my personal favourites are pistachios, but any type will do. They are full of protein and will keep you away from sugary alternatives.
2. **Lentil bites** – these are great if you love crisps. They are just as tasty and much healthier.
3. **Flavoured water supplements** – these are brilliant for providing you with the right amount of vitamins at the start of the day.
4. **Fruit** – dried or fresh. Swap your sweet treats for this healthier option to avoid the sugar slump that often follows a chocolate attack.
5. **Granola and yoghurt** – this snack is perfect at break time as it keeps you going until lunch time with its energy-releasing goodness.
6. **Water** – an obvious one but how many glasses do you actually drink a day? Often when we think we are hungry, we may only need a drink. Infuse your water with fruits for a better flavour.
7. **Fruit tea** – this stuff works wonders. Find a flavour that suits you, but generally any green tea flavour is great for the digestive system.
8. **Mints** – great when you need a burst of freshness after lunch.

> **Next steps**
> Why not shop for the week and make all your lunches in advance at the weekend? I started doing this recently and it has transformed my eating habits. By choosing healthy, filling options and making sure I have a healthy breakfast, I automatically have more energy throughout the day.

#snackattack
#notice

Idea 5: Wellbeing MOT

Taking the time to assess your wellbeing is crucial.

How do you know when you've taken on too much and are struggling? Sometimes, we need to take a step back and reflect on our workload and our day-to-day working lives. One of the ways in which I do this is by taking some time to ask myself some important questions. A pen and paper, and the right thinking, can often be all you need to set things straight in your head. Use these ten questions to assess your current wellbeing. If your answer to any of them concerns you, consider taking steps to change something and alleviate the pressure. What one thing could you change to see a difference, however small it may be?

1. Are you sleeping six to eight hours a night?
2. Have you worked over your paid hours this week?
3. Do you have downtime in the evenings that doesn't involve work?
4. Are you eating healthily?
5. Do you drink enough water each day?
6. Do you regularly work on weekends?
7. Do you spend regular quality time with your family and friends?
8. Do you have time alone to relax?
9. Do you feel overwhelmed with your workload?
10. Do you have someone to talk to about your concerns?

Next steps

Obviously I am not a professional doctor and the above advice is simply to get you thinking about the basic needs of a human body. As teachers, we are renowned for putting others first, often at the detriment of our own wellbeing. It's okay to put yourself first. If you do feel like you are too stressed, please make sure you act upon it before it gets any worse.

A practical approach to this could be to keep a log of your working hours over a week or two and if you find you are significantly over your paid hours, take action and make changes to alleviate the pressure. Remember, your health is more important than your next lesson plan.

#wellbeingMOT
#connect
#learn

Idea 6: Postcard promise

Planning and managing your wellbeing goals will keep the balance right throughout the year.

In order to maintain a healthy balance between your work and social life, you need to be proactive. That means taking control right from the start and reflecting on your wellbeing all the way through the year.

This year, I made myself a promise to do three things. I try to stand by these at all times. They are:

1. Leave work early at least once a week.
2. Challenge workload that has little impact on pupil progress but a significant impact on teacher time.
3. Understand that it's okay to say no.

I wrote these down on a postcard and stuck them on the wall in my office as a constant reminder. So far, it's worked really well. I chose a Wednesday to go home early and I don't work at all that evening. It feels like a mini weekend and splits the week up nicely. I did indeed challenge a marking policy that was driving me into the ground. As a result, a new policy was drafted and this had a huge impact on my time and resulted in greater progress for pupils too. The final maxim is a little more difficult for me at times, as I'm a people pleaser by nature. I am, however, making sure I say no sometimes.

Have a go at creating your own wellbeing maxims and make sure they are visible somewhere that you will see them every day.

> **Next steps**
> Write yourself a letter about how you are going to manage your wellbeing over the academic year. It could also contain what you hope to achieve by the end of the year. Place it in an envelope and hand it to someone you trust. Tell them to post it to you at the end of the year and see if you managed to stick to it. Taking time to reflect at the end of the year will also enable you to reassess your priorities too.

#postcardpromise
#connect
#volunteer
#teacher5aday
#nurture

Idea 7: Club classics

Taking time to socialise with colleagues improves your wellbeing.

At my school, there are a number of events taking place to encourage staff to get together, socialise, share interests and boost wellbeing. The great thing about them is that they are all so different. Below are just some of the ideas that you or your school could set up.

Running club
During the spring and summer term, create a staff and pupil running club. Ours takes place on a Wednesday morning before school, and participants run about a mile. The staff feel energised for the day and the pupils love taking part too.

Teaching and learning club
For a more academic morning, this is a club where teachers turn up to listen to a colleague share their best teaching and learning idea. The session is led by someone different each week and teachers know when their slot is well in advance. For secondary teachers, this is great for discussing topics with those outside of your subject area.

Book club
This is my personal favourite. Every half term, I lead a staff book club that attracts colleagues from all over the school, including support staff. We nominate books, and titles are drawn out of a hat. The time spent discussing the books and sharing tea and cake is simply wonderful. It provides a necessary oasis in the middle of what is usually a busy week.

Choir club
Starting a staff choir is yet another way to bring colleagues together and do something that isn't necessarily related to their everyday role. Vocal chords at the ready, everyone!

#clubclassics
#connect

> **Next steps**
> To set up your own club, send out a message on the school bulletin; if you get enough interest, try to set up a club that runs at least six times across the year. Not only will this benefit your own wellbeing, you'll be contributing to improving the wellbeing of others too.

Idea 8: Just say no

Being able to say no to unreasonable requests is empowering and keeps your wellbeing in check.

When I started at a new school two years ago, I was asked to take on a number of whole-school responsibilities. Every time I agreed, I wondered how I was going to manage my workload, yet I still said yes. Why? Because I didn't want to let anyone down. I wanted to appear keen and willing. You can probably guess where I'm going with this. In the end, I couldn't do all the roles as well as I would have liked, as there simply wasn't enough time. It took a long time for me to realise that it is okay to say no. Yes, it's difficult, but the next time you are asked to take on extra responsibility, ask yourself the following three questions.

1. Is it part of your job description?
In my example above, I actually ended up with a variety of responsibilities that ranged from developing a reading culture to managing NQTs. The problem was that they were all large responsibilities that needed time to be done well. The other issue was that they didn't really fit very well together. When you are taking on extra responsibility, make sure it fits with your skills and expertise. If it's not even relevant to your job description, should you be doing it?

2. Will you have time to do it well during normal working hours?
This is important, as if you do take on extra work, you must have time to be able to do it well. That doesn't mean extra hours at the weekend or after work during the week. That's your downtime. If you are honestly working at capacity already, ask yourself whether you can afford to sacrifice your wellbeing in order to take on this new role.

3. What will be taken from you in order for you to effectively manage the new responsibility?
This question ties in with the previous one. If you really want to take on the new role but are at capacity already, negotiate. Ask your line manager to take something else away from you. If they are supportive, they'll agree to your very reasonable request. If they say no, consider whether the role was right for you in the first place. Do you really want to take

on a role that you know will negatively impact your wellbeing? It's okay to turn down the role if this is the case.

If and when you do find the power to say no, you will be rewarded with a number of benefits.

Firstly, you'll have more time to do your current role properly. There won't be any additional responsibilities that you feel you cannot manage.

Secondly, you will feel far more empowered and authentic than if you had agreed to the additional responsibility and struggled to keep up with the workload. Controlling your own workload is something that makes you feel empowered to do things well. It also ensure that you stay true to yourself and your goals at work.

Thirdly, your productivity will improve. You will feel like you are much more capable of doing the role you agreed to. You realise just how precious your time is and that makes you more productive in the time you have to work.

You are also far better at making decisions and far more self-disciplined. If you are committed to not saying yes to everything, it means you think before you act, which leads to better decisions. Not only that, it takes a lot to say no to someone who is in a position of authority over you. Once you have done so, you have practised the skill of self-discipline, which will only get stronger the more you learn to say no in favour of better wellbeing. Just make sure you explain your reasons to the person asking the request so they know you have good intentions.

> **Next steps**
> If you have them, use your performance management meetings and targets to highlight your areas of interest. That way, you are more likely to be asked to take on responsibilities that you are invested in and may already have experience in.

**#justsayno
#notice
#learn**

Idea 9: SOS box

Planning ahead is important in such a busy role.

Do you ever get to a point in the year when you really need something during the school day but just don't have it to hand? This happens to me all the time! At the start of term, try putting together a teacher SOS box with all the items you need at work on a regular basis. The following items could be included in your box:

- **Hand cream** – for the winter months when your hands are feeling the wear and tear of teacher life.
- **Hand sanitiser** – there should never be a reason not to have some of this magic stuff.
- **Safety pins** – I guarantee you will be asked by a pupil for one of these at some point in your career.
- **Paper clips, treasury tags or elastic bands** – a small stash of these could prove vital to keeping important papers together.
- **Drawing pins** – if you like displays, you'll need some of these to keep them tidy.
- **Painkillers** – keep some of these handy in case you have a killer headache attack (obviously, keep them out of reach of small hands).
- **Plasters** – paper cuts are part and parcel of working in a school so a handful of these won't go amiss.
- **Tissues** – for those times when you need to dry a tear or blow a nose or two.
- **Throat sweets** – your voice is one of the most important tools you have as a teacher. Keep it safe and look after it when it gets tired or sore.
- **Marking pens** – how many times have you had teachers ask you for a spare one or have you needed one for yourself? If you regularly keep your stock topped up and have some in the SOS box, you're winning.
- **Mints** – who doesn't need to freshen up during the day?

Next steps

Create an SOS box for your faculty area or department team. They will love the idea and it creates a supportive team environment if colleagues know you care about their wellbeing.

#SOSbox
#notice

Idea 10: Rainy day retrieval

It's important to recognise your value even when you don't feel like it.

Picture this: it's a dark November day in the middle of a busy term. You've had to deal with difficult situations all day. First, the copier breaks and you lambast yourself for not preparing your resources the day before. Second, a child is disruptive in your lesson and it causes other pupils to misbehave. Third, you forget your duty as you are trying to get your resources sorted. Fourth, a disgruntled parent calls in to discuss why their child has been given a detention. Fifth, you realise your lunch is sitting in your fridge at home. Okay, so this is an extreme example, but we've all had days that have left us feeling utterly useless. Teachers suffer from 'imposter syndrome' at the best of times, even without all these added complications getting involved. For those of you unfamiliar with the term 'imposter syndrome', it involves high-achieving individuals who are unable to recognise their successes, so feel like a 'fraud' and fear constantly that they will be 'found out'. In layman's terms, it's thinking and feeling you aren't good enough.

One way in which you could counteract this feeling is to collect 'thank you' messages. Try keeping emails of thanks in a folder of their own. Save cards and notes from colleagues, parents and pupils in a box. Whenever you're having a bad day, simply take ten minutes to look at them. It will help to remind you that you're not as bad as you think you are and will be a real confidence boost when you need it most.

> **Next steps**
> At the end of each day, write down five things you are proud of and store these somewhere. This will encourage you to focus on the positives of the day and you can refer back to them whenever you need a reminder of how incredible you are. And, trust me, you are amazing.

#rainyday
#notice
#learn

Idea 11: Mini weekend

Making time for yourself mid-week really does make a huge difference.

One of the best things I did recently to improve my work–life balance was to introduce a mini weekend for myself in the middle of my working week. The idea is simple: once a week, every week, you go home early and do no work whatsoever once you get there. This idea does take some getting used to and it also requires some forward planning.

In order to enjoy your night off, you need to make sure everything is in place for the rest of the week. My early day is a Wednesday, so every Monday or Tuesday I make sure that my lessons, resources and tasks for Thursday and Friday are ready. This means I can go home as early as possible on Wednesday and do whatever I like once I'm there. It is pure, guilt-free downtime that I just wasn't making time for previously. I couldn't believe the difference it made.

This one change has the potential to have a significant impact on your wellbeing. You will feel like you've had a good rest and some time away from work-related matters. It also allows you to refocus your time on those you care about outside of work. You are suddenly able to make time to call that friend you've been meaning to catch up with or arrange the visit to your parents you've been planning for some time. Those of you with partners will also see benefits, as you will have more time to spend with them. A final benefit of this idea is that upon your return to work, you will feel much brighter and fresher, ready to make excellent progress with your pupils.

#myminiweekend
#connect
#notice

Next steps
Once a month, arrange a mid-week night out. It doesn't matter who it's with, just make sure you have one planned. Arrange it even if you don't feel like it. It can be all too easy to become bogged down with work. Feeling exhausted can make you want to stay in all the time, but to break the cycle, you must make the effort to go out, and once you're there, I'm positive you'll be glad you arranged it. Remember, you won't have to worry about the rest of the working week, as you'll have already planned it all!

Idea 12: Declutter days

Decluttering clears space in your room and in your mind.

The benefits of decluttering have been talked and written about for years now. Whether it be decluttering your house or even your 'friends list' on Facebook, it can have a powerful impact on your wellbeing. Here's how it could be used in teaching:

Declutter your work desk. If you're anything like me, you'll have a mountain of paper on your desk at the end of every day. Don't leave the classroom until it has all been filed or recycled.

Declutter your emails. Make sure that all your emails are filed or deleted by the end of every day, so that your inbox is empty in the morning (unless you've received more through the evening of course). This works wonders for wellbeing, as each day you start afresh. For more on managing your inbox, see Idea 28.

Declutter your files. A messy desktop or folder system can be damaging to your wellbeing. Remove any unused resources and store them externally. This will keep things tidy and ensure you can find things much more quickly.

Declutter your school cupboards. I tend to do this at the end of a term. It makes sense to keep only the resources you need or you'll end up with stacks of paperwork that isn't used. It's also incredibly cathartic to have a good old clear out.

Declutter your work wardrobe. This is something I do at the end of each academic year. I often find clothes I've either never worn or completely overused. Having a clear out makes way for some new items that will make you feel good at the start of a new year. How you feel in your work clothes can have a significant impact on your wellbeing.

> **Next steps**
> Become clutter-free as a whole department or school by building in 'declutter time' on training days, during which everyone takes part in making the school a clutter-free space.

#declutterdays
#notice

Idea 13: Take a break

Taking a break from the pressures of work is vital to your wellbeing.

This seems like an obvious idea, but in all honesty how many of us actually take the time to have a real break from all things work? Teachers are notoriously bad at downing tools and logging out. As a new teacher, I remember working horrific hours and wasting any opportunity of a rest at the weekend by trying to plan everything for the following week. That kind of lifestyle is simply not sustainable and is where many teachers go wrong. It's a quick path to burnout and illness. Force yourself if you have to, but please, please, please take a break. Here are some ways you can switch off:

1. Take an actual weekend break. In advance, book a weekend away in the middle of a term. Just do it. Once it's booked, there's no way you can cancel and it really will allow you some time away from the stresses of work. And don't allow yourself to feel guilty for taking some time out. It's ridiculous that we spend a significant amount of time at work and then feel guilty for not doing more work during what is supposed to be our own free time.

2. If you want to really improve your wellbeing, book a retreat. I met a lovely lady called Lizzie Fouracre whilst staying in a hostel in Snowdonia (during term time), who had left her well-paid, successful job behind in search of something more valuable to her. She now owns a business called The Humble Retreat. It's a place where weary workers can go to receive a whole weekend of pure relaxation, including yoga, wholesome food and stunning walks. Lizzie is an inspiring lady and her retreat is well worth a visit! You can find her on Facebook here: @thehumbleretreat

3. Take a break from weekend planning. Put down the books. Leave the laptop at work. Don't do anything work-related. You'll feel all the more refreshed for it in the long run. Aim to do this once a half term.

4. Take a digital break. Don't use your computer or phone for the entire weekend. Don't check Twitter. Ban all social media sites. Often our brains are working overtime because of the amount of time we spend staring at our phones. Reconnect with yourself, family, friends or even a good book, but leave the technology behind.

#takeabreak
#connect

Chapter 2

Recognition mission

Looking after those around you is just as important as taking care of your own wellbeing.

I have been lucky to work in schools where I have been part of a fully supportive, fantastic bunch of teachers, but I've also worked in schools where the complete opposite was the case. The latter was pretty awful and not something I want to experience again in the future. I see schools as microcosms of society, each working towards the same common goal of supporting pupils in the best way possible. Whilst pupil progress is paramount to a school's success, it's also important that this goal is replicated when we think about our colleagues. They too need support when the days are tough. There have been times when I simply wouldn't have got through a day if it wasn't for the generosity and kindness of my colleagues. This is something I feel vehemently about. Luckily, it doesn't take much to let a colleague know you are there for them. This chapter is packed with ideas about how to support your colleagues and show that you appreciate them and the work they do. Great schools exist because teams work well together. See if you can find an idea to try this week. I would love to hear what you do!

Idea 14: Wellbeing bags

Wellbeing bags visibly lift the atmosphere in the staffroom.

Create a wellbeing bag for anyone you think deserves recognition and a pick-me-up for their hard work and commitment. What better way to show someone you care about their wellbeing and appreciate their efforts than by giving them a goody bag full of items that will boost their energy and revive their thinking?

This idea came about as a 'thank you' to staff for taking part in a TeachMeet held in my school as part of our CPD programme. The wellbeing bags were gratefully received and talked about for months afterwards. Since then, I have seen many versions of the bags on Twitter with all kinds of items inside.

Here are some items that could be included in the bags:

- **Sticky notes** – to leave praise for other staff members when they least expect it.
- **Chocolate** – for a sweet pick-me-up at the end of a long day.
- **Stickers** – to make marking and planning easier.
- **Notepad** – to jot great ideas down when you're on the go.
- **Biscuits** – to offer to everyone on duty.
- **Highlighters** – to identify the best lessons in your planning.
- **Tea** – to keep you going during the colder terms.
- **Mints** – to keep you cool and calm in meetings.
- **A baking book** – so you can set up a baking rota for your staff meetings.
- **Thank you cards** – these can be used by the person receiving the wellbeing bag. They can send them round so they can thank people too. Pay-it-forward initiatives work well in schools.
- **Pens** – every teacher I know loves stationery. Why not add some fancy pens to the bag and add some colour to a teacher's notetaking?
- **Tissues** – for those cold morning duty days.

You can be as creative as you like with your wellbeing bags, by using themes or having a particular focus such as healthy living or teaching and learning. Search for #wellbeingbags on Twitter for plenty of inspiration.

Anyone can make the bags too; you can be a school leader who makes them for the entire staff or a teacher who wants to thank an individual person. Their adaptability is what makes them so popular.

If you're short on funding, contact local businesses for sponsorship. Plenty of them will gladly support you in your quest to improve teacher wellbeing.

#wellbeingbags
#volunteer
#connect

> ## Next steps
> Why not create wellbeing revision kits for pupils? I first saw this idea on Twitter when Lesley Munroe shared her 'revision survival kits'. They are a simple adaptation of the staff wellbeing bags with slight changes to the contents. Items such as a revision timetable, revision tips and key facts cards can be added, alongside the sweet treats and stationery.

Idea 15: Wellbeing winners

Winning a wellbeing prize makes you feel valued.

Create a wellbeing nomination box. Every week, ask staff to nominate someone who they feel is deserving of a wellbeing prize. It can be for anything at all, like covering someone's break duty or lesson, for example. Perhaps someone has simply been a listening ear at the end of a tough day. This idea stemmed from wellbeing bags (see Idea 14) but it affects a greater number of people on a weekly basis. It includes all staff members from senior leadership to site staff. During weekly briefing, have someone draw a name from the wellbeing nomination box, read out the reason for their nomination and give them the prize.

Once the prize has been awarded, all the nominations can be shared on a display board in the staffroom. This means that everyone can see who was nominated and what they did to deserve a nomination. It's a lovely way to show how much everyone has done for each other over the week. This creates a sense of cohesion and it's great to see staff taking part, nominating colleagues and reading the display board. You could even send an email to all those nominated to really make their day.

There are many versions of these recognition boards. Amjad Ali (@ ASTsupportAAli), a wonderful teacher who has a teaching and learning toolkit at www.trythisteaching.com, shared it as a 'staff shout out' board, where staff could add messages to thank colleagues at any time.

Another variation of this idea is to have a wellbeing cup that members of staff have the opportunity to win each week. This idea is slightly different in that the person who wins the prize gets to nominate a new person the following week. The cup is then passed on from the previous winner to their newly nominated winner. Simple yet effective; it keeps everyone on their toes!

Next steps

Place mini wellbeing prizes in your colleagues' pigeon-holes when they least expect it. The effort is minimal and the reaction you get is well worth it. There's something quite lovely about receiving a little treat totally by surprise.

#wellbeingwinners
#notice
#volunteer

Idea 16: Secret wellbeing buddies

The secrecy behind this idea is part of the fun.

I first learned about this idea on Twitter. A wonderful primary head-teacher by the name of Nicola Wood (@NicolaWood54) wanted to improve wellbeing in her school and show staff they are valued. At the start of the year, she asked all staff members to fill in a questionnaire about themselves. The questionnaires were collated and staff were allocated a 'secret wellbeing buddy' and given that staff member's questionnaire. Those who wished to take part were told that it was their responsibility to support that person throughout the year by sending them small gifts, notes or cards to let them know they were valued. With the questionnaire detailing their likes and dislikes, the 'secret buddy' knows exactly what treats would be best to give to their 'secret buddy'. At the end of the year, the mystery of 'who was who' is revealed and the sense of community is strengthened.

A similar idea was created by a teacher called Victoria Hewitt (@MrsHumanities). Victoria asks Twitter users to sign up to a #Back2School buddy box scheme. If you sign up, you are assigned a buddy, who then sends you a buddy box full of goodies at the start of the new academic year. In addition, you can nominate someone who you feel deserves a buddy box upon their return to work. It's a wonderful scheme, which has created many smiles over the school year. This idea would also be great at a local level. Schools could buddy up with other local schools and devise a buddy system to take place across the year. Each term, buddy boxes could be sent to other schools. It's a great way to improve wellbeing and strengthen community links too.

#wellbeingbuddies
#volunteer

Next steps

Last year, I sent out a significant number of wellbeing bags to people whom I had met at teaching conferences and through Twitter. They didn't know they were being sent anything and it was a total surprise when they received them. Not only does this make others feel valued, but it boosts your own wellbeing too. Random acts of kindness really do go down well!

Idea 17: The power of a name

Knowing the names of those you work with ensures they feel valued and saves you a lot of time too!

This idea may seem a little obvious, but it's a quick win to encouraging teacher wellbeing. Not only does it ensure people feel recognised but it also means things can be actioned much more quickly. To add an anecdotal example, I know of two teachers who are continuously mixed up by other teachers. They share the same first name (spelt differently) and are forever being sent the wrong emails by staff. It actually borders on insulting. Knowing the names of those you work with ensures they feel valued and recognised, which in turn supports their wellbeing.

Without knowing everyone's name, from pupils in your classes to teaching staff right through to support staff, everything also becomes just a little bit more difficult, not to mention time-consuming. How are you going to send an email to the SENDCo if you don't know their name? How will you book the hall if you don't know the name of the site manager? How will you stop a pupil to praise them or redirect them if you don't know who they are? As you can see, being unaware of names can cause a considerable amount of unnecessary stress for you and everyone else around you. When you consider the number of names a teacher has to remember each year, the problem seems to get bigger. Secondary school teachers have to remember over a hundred names each year and that's just the pupils!

So, what can you do about it? Learn their names quickly, of course! Here are some useful tips to get you remembering those names more quickly:

- **Name tags**: Don't be afraid to use name tags in your classes for the first couple of weeks.
- **Seating plans**: Making sure you have a seating plan will speed up the name recollection instantly.
- **Register games**: Use taking the register to help you remember pupils' names. Ask them to add an adjective to their name, like 'Amazing Amy', for example. You are more likely to remember them if you add a bit of their personality to their names.

- **Staff list**: Ask for a full staff list at the start of the year and try to link names with faces at every opportunity.
- **Visual images**: Create visual images of places where you are likely to find certain people. By grouping them into different areas, you will increase the likelihood of remembering their names. Association is a powerful memory tool.
- **Say it aloud**: Use a person's name as you speak with them, as you are more likely to remember it if you say it out loud. Repeat it as often as you can. This also has the added bonus of making the person you are talking to feel valued, as you know them well enough to refer to them by name.
- **Break times**: Get out and about during break times and lunch times to speak to as many people as you can. The more you interact with different staff members outside of your area, the quicker you will get to know them and their names.

#learnthosenames
#learn

Idea 18: Cover care

Offering your time to cover someone never goes unnoticed.

Schools are busy places and they work most successfully when everyone is rowing in the same direction. Some of the best schools I've ever worked in or visited have been those where the staff and pupils visibly support each other when they can. There have been times when I have needed to observe another teacher's lesson or attend a training event and have only been able to do so because of the kindness of those around me. If you understand how schools operate, then you'll understand why it's so important to offer your help to colleagues where possible. Here are some things you can do to show your support.

You could offer to take a colleague's break or lunch duty. There are many reasons why a colleague might need some support here. They could be feeling unwell or dealing with a pupil, or they might need to call a parent. They might even be visibly exhausted and you happen to have noticed. Taking their duty for them goes a long way even if you are simply saving them 20 minutes.

You could even offer to take someone's lesson for them. Again, there could be a myriad of reasons why this kind of support is needed, but the important thing to remember is that your gesture won't go unnoticed and, as a bonus, you'll feel much better about yourself for doing it too!

The above advice includes other types of support: covering a revision session, covering a detention duty or even taking the place of a colleague on a school trip. Without these gestures, schools become inflexible places and there will undoubtedly be a time when you need the favour returning.

Next steps

Sometimes, a little more than offering cover is needed. In the past, I have offered to mark some of my colleagues' work due to them having personal issues affecting their performance. This is, of course, a greater responsibility for you and a big ask, but you are releasing a bigger amount of weight for the person you are helping and you can be sure they'll appreciate the support. Why not go the extra mile for your colleagues every once in a while?

#covercare
#volunteer
#connect

Idea 19: The [insert school name here] Bake Off

Cooking competitions lighten the working week and encourage downtime in the evenings.

One of the best things about working in schools is that you become part of a community of people. The best places to work bring people together in many ways. At one school I worked at, we had a competition in the style of *The Great British Bake Off*, which I thought was a brilliant idea. It encouraged staff to focus on their wellbeing by promoting downtime and relaxation instead of evening planning and marking, whilst also bringing together staff who wouldn't normally communicate in their day-to-day working lives. Plus, who doesn't like a bit of competition? Why not set up a similar idea in your own school? Here are some ideas of how it could work:

- At a whole-school level, ask staff to sign up at the beginning of the year. Begin your competition in the first term and have six rounds, one for every half term. Offer a prize to the winners of each round and maybe a smaller prize for those who took part too. Everyone loves a certificate, especially teachers!
- Select a theme for each term to give your competitors some direction. (Ensure you have a balance of healthy versus less so.)
- Make sure the rest of the school knows it's taking place – the more recognition staff get for taking part, the more likely others are to sign up next time around.

#bakeoffchallenge
#connect
#notice

Next steps
Why not set up a baking rota within your smaller teams? Each time you have a meeting, make it someone's responsibility to bring in a homemade snack. Anyone who isn't exactly a culinary expert can bring in shop-bought goodies. What does it matter when you're supporting the wellbeing of your team?

Idea 20: The power of 'thank you'

Saying thank you to someone has more impact than you realise.

For as long as I can remember, I have always felt particularly wonderful about things I have done when I've received a 'thank you' from someone for doing them. Of course, that isn't the reason we want to work hard, but the power those two little words can have is immense. As teachers, we are often overworked and it can be difficult to step out from our own work bubble to recognise the great things that our colleagues are doing on a daily basis. Actually, when you stop and think about it, all it takes is five to ten minutes of your week to show staff that you appreciate their efforts. Some of my most supportive line managers have done just that in many different ways. Here are just a few ways in which you can say thank you:

- **Cards or postcards**: Buy a stash of these at the beginning of the year and send them out to unsuspecting colleagues each week to say thank you. I love receiving these. I stick them up somewhere noticeable as a reminder of how valued I am, and it's nice to see them grow in number over the school year.
- **Sweet treats**: This has already been mentioned in Idea 16: Secret wellbeing buddies, except this time, let your colleague know who has left it and why.
- **The Big Five**: Send five thank you messages out to people who deserve the credit each week. It doesn't matter how you do it, as long as the message gets to them. I send thank you emails often. There have been so many times I've felt really valued because someone has taken the time to send me a thank you email.
- **Sticky notes**: This is one of the quickest ways to show people you appreciate them. Leave little thank you sticky notes for those who deserve it in their classroom or at their seat in the staffroom.

The best way to be effective with this idea is to send the 'thank you' out as soon as you remember, or make a little note throughout the week of who you think deserves a 'thank you' and send them all at once. Avoid setting aside time on a Friday to do it, as it's easy to forget to send them. Save it until Monday, when you can send them out straight away. What better feeling for someone to have than opening their emails or checking their pigeonhole on a Monday morning and finding a lovely thank you message in there?

It's worth mentioning that it's not only people you work closely with who deserve a thank you note. More recently, I have been particularly perceptive at spotting when staff members are having a bad day. It's usually in the corridor that I spot them. They may not be their usual perky self, or could even be short and snappy. It would be easy to take offence to this kind of behaviour and to avoid that person for a while, but we've all had days like that. These are the people who would benefit the most from a note to check on their wellbeing. Dropping a postcard into their pigeon hole to let them know you care really does work wonders. Why not try it for yourself and see what happens?

#saythankyou
#connect
#volunteer

Idea 21: Sharing good practice

Developing those around you and recognising their effort and skill promotes wellbeing.

At a previous school, my Head of Faculty, Fiona McCluskey, was absolutely brilliant at promoting her staff, so much so that we all felt valued and respected. One of the ways in which she supported us and showed she valued our teaching was to ask us to share our best practice at the start of every faculty meeting. At every meeting, everyone was given the chance to share something that had worked for them that week. Not only did it boost our confidence individually, but it also showed a respect for our skill as teachers. Another positive was that we started every single meeting on a high. We naturally felt good about our week and avoided the very easy tendency to moan about things that had happened. As teachers and members of a team, we have a responsibility to shield each other from the negativity that can all too often surround our profession. This idea was a subtle reminder to us all about what is important: the pupils and great teaching and learning.

This constant support and promotion extended far beyond our faculty team. Whenever there was an opportunity to praise us as a team, it was taken up by this wonderful lady. Often we would receive messages of thanks and congratulations from other members of the school community for something we had done that week too. We always knew they could only have found out from Fiona.

Why not try sharing teaching and learning ideas at the start of your next staff meeting or considering other ways in which you can share best practice whilst also boosting your colleagues' moods?

#sharingmypractice
#volunteer
#connect

Next steps
A great way to develop this further is to have a list of everyone's teaching and learning ideas compiled and shared with all staff. Encourage staff to try the ideas that worked well for their colleagues and report back in meetings. This keeps the focus on developing great teaching and learning but also contributes to the sense of pride staff might feel knowing someone else has tried their idea.

Idea 22: Shadow support

Supporting colleagues with difficult pupils can be a huge help.

We've all been there. The nightmare class. The one pupil you just don't want to deal with but who you know will be in because he never misses a day! Over the years, I have had to deal with some very difficult classes. At times, it's left me feeling quite low. As my teaching experience developed, I became much better at behaviour management, but one of the things I remember most clearly about those difficult days was just how supportive colleagues were, and equally just how unsupportive others could be.

If you feel confident with your behaviour management, try offering some shadow support to a colleague. The idea is that you offer to help your colleague in any way you can, and as such, you are recognising that teams work better together. Here are just some of the ways you could offer support:

- Agree to be part of an errand task. Sending a difficult pupil on an 'important errand' at the start of a lesson can allow a teacher vital time to settle the rest of the class and start on the work with no disruptions. Offer to receive the said pupil to help your colleague out.
- Offer support in class. The last thing any teacher has an abundance of is time, but by offering to support a teacher with a particularly difficult class, you are showing you care and the favour will be repaid when you need it most. It doesn't have to be for the whole lesson – you could just pop your head in from time to time. Eventually, the pupils click on to the situation and decide it isn't worth the hassle.
- Set up a shadow timetable. This is a planned approach to shadowing, which can work amazingly well. A timetable is drawn up (by the head of department or the appropriate leader), which shadows the main timetable of lessons. Teachers are able to send a problematic pupil to another class if they become too disruptive in the lesson. Every teacher takes part and is expected to host the pupil sent to them for the rest of that lesson. This idea really shows how effective a supportive team can be and it's a godsend to new or less experienced teachers.

#shadowsupport
#connect
#volunteer

Idea 23: Come dine with me, teacher

Recognising the need to come together as a team strengthens working relationships.

This is an idea that can really bring a team together to help strengthen working relationships. In the style of the television programme *Come Dine With Me*, the team comes together one night every half term outside of school and the work environment and, you guessed it, one person cooks the others a meal. It's a simple idea that works.

Here's a suggested format:

- Before the event itself, take notes on the great things everyone has done at work. You will need these for the first event. Remember that the nights are all about recognising the power of being a strong team. Appreciation is a big part of that.
- If you don't know your team too well, be sure to pick up on their likes and dislikes as the first term develops. This will give you a good idea of what prizes to buy. A personal touch to the prizes will mean the sentiment goes further.
- Take the hit and be the first to host. It shows you are willing and you get a chance to model how you want the evening to run. If you aren't a fan of having people round to your home, or it isn't big enough, host the event at a local pub or restaurant. Okay, so you may not have cooked, but you are hosting the event, which is the important bit. Besides, there's nothing to say you can't make a dessert and share that with everyone!
- During the night, award prizes to everyone for the effort they have put in over the half term. Explain why they have won and show your appreciation publicly. A little 'thank you' really does go a long way.
- Once the first event is over, draw names from a hat and let everyone know which half term they have been allocated. Give them plenty of time and don't forget to send timely reminders, as it is so easy to become bogged down with the day-to-day workload of teaching life.
- If there are more of you than there are half terms, it's a perfect opportunity to double up and get planning together. This will encourage even more team spirit.

If a half-termly event seems a little too often, why not try it termly instead? Meeting with your team three times a year is just as good for building strong relationships. It's also worth considering what already takes place at the school where you work. The school I currently work at is quite sociable. We regularly hold whole-staff social events that are well attended. I've come to look forward to such events and obviously they are optional, so there's no real pressure to attend.

#comedinewithmeteacher
#connect
#notice

Next steps

Why not try to reach out to other departments or subject areas and team up? A little bit of competition never hurt anyone and who knows how many teams you could end up with!

Idea 24: Friday feeling

Celebrating each other's hard work and effort will leave everyone feeling valued at the end of a busy week.

Whenever I think about the hard work and effort that teachers put in on a daily basis, I am absolutely amazed. I have mentioned this before, but it's worth stating again. Schools really are run on the goodwill of teachers. We give up our time willingly to support the smooth running of the schools in which we work and to help the pupils we teach. Can you imagine what would happen if every teacher in the country decided to work their paid hours and nothing more? If every teacher in the country just said, 'No, that's it, I can't do it anymore'? What a shock it would be to all involved. Our effort is quite frankly above and beyond what is required every single day, every single week. Yet it has almost become an acceptance. A given. That is what teachers have always done so why bother discussing it? This is just plain wrong. We need to be shouting from the rooftops when we see teachers going above and beyond. Everyone should be on the lookout for the amazing extras that teachers do and, my goodness, we should all receive the accolade for our efforts. We do it for the pupils we teach, so why not do it for each other?

Now, that kind of revolution isn't going to happen overnight but as individuals we can all try to start somewhere. We can all be doing more to recognise each other's successes.

Friday feeling is an idea that can be run as a department or small team. Basically, the idea is that the team comes together at the end of the school day every Friday to celebrate each other's efforts. Each member of staff will have the opportunity to praise and thank another member of the team for something they have done that week. It doesn't have to be something they did for them, just something they noticed another member of staff do that they think deserves a thank you.

There are several benefits to this idea. Firstly, it means that everyone receives some praise for their hard work. This will leave them feeling proud of their accomplishments, even if they thought they'd had a bad week, as someone else has recognised a positive for them. This means that everyone will leave for the weekend with a sense of achievement, whether their week was a good one or not. What a powerful thought. Secondly, it brings everyone together at the end of the week and strengthens the team you work in. Teaching is often a solitary job, despite the fact we spend our time in the presence of others all day. Often, you may not see another member of your team all week, which can lead to feelings of isolation. Friday feeling avoids that. Finally, it encourages a sense of purpose within a team. Everyone can see that you are all rowing together towards the same goal. It's a great feeling to know that you aren't the only one working hard and that you are part of a supportive team of people who recognise your efforts. Why not suggest it or give it a try yourself?

Next steps

Why not set up a much larger-scale Friday feeling in your school? Contact your headteacher or the person in charge of staff wellbeing (I really hope your school has one) and introduce the idea. Find a way in which everyone receives some sort of praise from someone else. It may take some setting up, but it isn't impossible to imagine. How nice would it be to receive an email from someone outside your department or immediate team, thanking you for something you have done that week? That kind of recognition is powerful and can really bring the school together as a whole.

Better still, start a trend of thanking people on Twitter for something they did that week. Encourage people to share the work of their colleagues on a national scale through social media. The more we celebrate teachers and their efforts, the better!

#Fridayfeeling
#notice
#connect

Idea 25: The little things

Taking the time every day to support your colleagues with the little things will go a long way.

As teachers, there are so many little things that we can do day in, day out to support each other. These little things are important and no less valuable than some of the bigger, more systematic practices that we can put in place. So, here these little things are, grouped together, but no less significant and in no particular order.

Praise staff to others
A simple one but how many times have you overheard staff having a moan about someone? Let's switch that around. If you are in a meeting and you have the opportunity to praise another staff member, do it. The world of education needs more of this.

Praise staff directly
Have they made a new display? Praise them. Have they shared in meetings? Praise them. You get the idea. There simply isn't enough of this praise stuff around. We could all be doing more of it.

Make time
It's easy to hide away in your room at work and never make time to see others. If you are one of those teachers, get up and get out. Go and talk to other teachers. It'll make them and you feel better. Likewise, if someone comes in for a chat with you, make the time if you can. We are all busy all of the time. We must make conscious decisions to support one another regardless.

Photocopying
We all have to do it, so why not do everyone's whilst you're at it? When this is done for me, I am genuinely grateful for the time it has saved me.

Drinks runs
Offer to make tea and coffee or get refreshments for your colleagues. I will always be happier when someone brings me coffee! Food runs also go down well. I love it when a colleague asks if I want anything from

the shop, even if it does mean I'll be eating naughty, unplanned treats that day.

Say hello to everyone in your team
In the morning, pop your head into everyone's classroom and say hello. It can be the difference between a good day and a bad day for that member of staff and costs you very little time. If you are feeling a little more generous with your time, ask how their weekend was. This can mean more than you know for some teachers.

#thelittlethings
#connect
#notice

Idea 26: Powerful positivity

Remaining positive when colleagues are having a bad day helps them see the wood for the trees.

In 2015, I was faced with a colleague who seemed to be eternally negative about pretty much everything. I couldn't understand how someone could be so gloomy all of the time. When I thought a bit harder about it, I realised that there are teachers like that all over the country. Every school has them. The mood hoover. The fun sponge. Whatever you want to call them, these are the people who seem to be in a perpetual state of misery. You'll hear them say: 'There's no milk left for my tea!' or 'I bet half the class hasn't done their homework' or 'I just know someone's going to kick off this afternoon.'

If there is something to complain about, they are the experts. If there is nothing to complain about, they'll still complain. They are definitely the people you should avoid, right?

Wrong.

In my humble opinion, I think they should be showered with kindness and support. I can tell you from experience that to feel unsupported is a really awful thing for anyone to deal with. So instead of avoiding them, we should be doing more of this:

'Here, have some of my milk' or 'Bring your best piece of homework to the meeting to share as good practice' or 'Shall we all try a crazy starter this afternoon to liven up our lessons?'

Positivity is contagious. It spreads like wildfire. Put simply, it works.

Schools are a community. That's what's so great about them. We don't know what personal battles people are fighting. So this idea is about supporting the people who need it the most in the hope that, in some small way, you make a difference.

#powerofpositivity
#connect
#notice

Chapter 3

Working smarter

Time-saving ideas for busy teachers.

This chapter is all about saving time. As teachers, time is precious to us and all too often we can become bogged down with tasks that simply take up too much of our time. Time is one of the things we value the most. I am often asked how I manage my time at work, as I still seem to have quite a busy social life. The answer is I prioritise my tasks and decide what is important and what can wait until the following week. Another suggestion that is important to note is that if you are already working at full capacity and you are asked to take on another task at work, answer in this way: 'Yes, I'm happy to do that, but what is it you would like me to *stop* doing instead?' This is a simple question that you are well within your rights to ask. Responsible leaders will respond positively to this. The fact is, if you are constantly running out of time to do the things you need to at work, this will negatively impact on your wellbeing and provide you with less time to have a social life. Precious time with family and friends should not suffer because workload is too high. The ideas within this chapter should help you save time and therefore improve your wellbeing. The chapter covers a variety of areas related to teaching, from marking and planning to simply being more efficient with emails. Dive in and see if you can make at least one change per term to earn yourself some more precious time.

Idea 27: Minimal marking

Using effective marking strategies will save you precious time.

In a Twitter poll I shared two years ago, I asked the question: 'Which of the following is the highest contributor to your workload?' The options were marking, planning, monitoring and tracking, and administrative tasks. With marking taking 56% of the 1,329 votes, it's clear more needs to be done to redress this issue. In 2016, Ofsted released the following statement: 'Ofsted does not expect to see any specific frequency, type or volume of marking and feedback; these are for the school to decide through its assessment policy.' (www.gov.uk/government/publications/school-inspection-handbook-from-september-2015/ofsted-inspections-mythbusting) Whilst many schools have taken this advice and actively sought to reduce the volume and frequency of marking, the advice in this idea is aimed at reducing marking time for teachers in schools where marking is still the most time-consuming task of a teacher's role.

Here are some little tips to help reduce marking time and increase efficiency:

- Ask pupils to place their books on your desk open on the page that was last marked, so you won't waste precious time wading through books to find the right page.
- Rank mock exams in order of the pupils' ability. Mark what is likely to be the lowest-scoring exam first and work your way up. Not only does this save time, as you won't spend time searching for a similar-marked response, but it also improves marking accuracy, as you are marking similar-ability responses together, rather than marking ad hoc.
- Place marking in the margin of a page rather than where the error is. This encourages pupils to find the error, whilst also saving you time as you won't be writing the same comment more than once for each line.
- 'Pink for think, green for great' – I was first introduced to this idea at a previous school. Highlight areas for improvement in pink and areas that are written well in green. This saves time and encourages pupils to focus on the pink areas to make progress.
- Use essay reflection sheets. Pupils complete these at the end of a mock exam. They must reflect on their written work by completing a series of tasks (often linked to assessment objectives). When you

collect them in for marking, they are much easier and quicker to mark because pupils have highlighted their strengths.

- Yellow box marking – this idea was first created at George Spencer Academy Trust. Teachers highlight a piece of writing that needs general improvement using a yellow highlighter. The pupils rewrite the work making improvements.
- Use peer- and self-assessment. Ask pupils to mark mini quizzes and tests to save you time. Train pupils to understand the mark schemes and have them mark short exam questions too.
- Mark in the morning. You are likely to get more done if you mark when you are at your most energetic and productive.
- Create a marking timetable, so you know which set of books you should be marking each week.
- Generate marking codes for commonly made mistakes. This can save time, as you won't be writing out the same target several times.
- Share marking responsibility across your team. Have expert markers of particular topics, papers or tasks. This increases consistency and saves time.
- Use external markers. This will not only save you time but also provide detailed feedback on the pupils' performance. It does come at a cost though! Companies like London Exam Marking Services offer this. A quick search through Google and you may find more local services.

#minimalmarking
#learn

Next steps

Why not tackle the issue head on and challenge the policies that have little impact on progress but take up too much precious teacher time? Be brave! Take a look at the marking policy adapted from the Michaela School in Idea 82 and see if it might work for your school.

Idea 28: Email efficiency

Managing your emails effectively will reduce your stress levels and save time.

What's the first thing you do when you arrive to work in the morning? Log on to the school system and, no doubt, check your emails. This can be disastrous for the day ahead as you are likely to get distracted by tasks and messages that arrived in your inbox overnight.

The solution to this?

Simple. Check your emails after you have set yourself up for the day. Avoid email sabotage by making sure you have all your resources ready for the day before you respond to messages. Not only does this save time in the morning, it also reduces the amount of pressure placed on you at the start of each day.

To save even more time, organise your folders too. You could organise them into the subjects you're teaching or the faculty you're part of, for example. Once you have read an email, decide if it needs filing or deleting. At the end of each day, make sure your inbox is empty. This encourages a feeling of completion and you'll feel far better if you keep a tidy inbox, rather than opening your emails to too much information.

Another great advantage of this is you will also save time when you need to find an important email sent previously. Gone are the days of endlessly searching through your disorganised inbox for a login username you forgot for the third time!

Whilst I'm on the topic of emails, why not set up a 'thank you' email folder too? When you're having a challenging day, it will feel good to read the kind messages you've received over the year and it acts as a reminder that you're making progress. See Idea 10 for more on this.

Next steps

Set up a folder just for the login and password details you need to access all the different school systems and databases. This will save you heaps of time.

#emailexpert
#connect
#learn

Idea 29: Booklet bonanza

Using booklets reduces planning time and allows for a consistent approach to teaching and learning.

If you hate using PowerPoint, this idea could be for you! The idea is that you create booklets instead of lesson-by-lesson PowerPoints, from which all pupils in the department can work. Admittedly, I still use PowerPoints with some of my classes, but I am slowly moving away from them. The booklets are based around a unit of work and can be planned by your head of department or collaboratively. They should cover the entire curriculum year and are best planned for each half term.

The main reasons for the change are twofold. Firstly, it allows all teachers to see the level of challenge required and the learning journey that the pupils will take, and it provides consistency across the department. Secondly, it saves teachers time. Once the booklets are complete, you will only ever need to adapt them if necessary.

Booklets also eliminate any time wasted at the beginning of a lesson when technology fails you. We've all been there, trying to set up the lesson, and the jazzy, all-singing, all-dancing, bells-ringing PowerPoint you made the night before just doesn't want to load or the format is wrong for some reason unbeknown to anyone. Having a pre-prepared booklet avoids this drama. It ensures a smooth and seamless start to your lesson. It's also worth noting that behaviour management could be improved by using booklets. Pupils become more focused on you and the task at hand and less focused on the whiteboard or screen that pretty much tells them everything you could say verbally anyway. Booklets avoid unwanted distraction by stripping lessons back to the basics and keeping pupils focused on the most important aspect of every lesson: the learning.

> **Next steps**
> Why not suggest trying out a booklet-based department in your own school? Perhaps it could be trialled with one class or even a whole key stage? If the school is reluctant, a trial may show the benefits by comparing the progress of pupils using booklets and those who do not.

#bookletbonanza
#learn

Idea 30: Technology time savers

Using technology to support learning can save you hours of time.

Over the years, I have come across quite a few technological ways of making my planning quicker, as well as enhancing the learning of the pupils in my class. Below are some of the websites or apps that I think are most useful and I would suggest you try out too.

- **Kahoot** (www.kahoot.com): This is an online quiz website. Open up an account and search for quizzes relevant to the topic you are teaching. There are thousands of them and they can be accessed instantly, saving you precious time. These are great for introducing a topic or for revision lessons. Just make sure you check every question before playing it with the pupils. If you're feeling really brave, you can make your own quiz and store it so you can use it multiple times over the years.
- **QR codes**: These have been around for a while now. They are digital barcodes that, when linked to information, can be scanned and the desired information will appear. If you ever want your pupils to access information quickly, this is a great way to do it. Try www.qrstuff.com to make your own.
- **Class Dojo** (www.classdojo.com): This is a communication app that works well in primary schools. It allows teachers to connect with parents and pupils using photos, videos and messages throughout the school day. It allows parents access to their child's progress instantly and works well to create supportive bonds between schools and pupils' families. The design of this app is one of its appealing aspects too; it's bright, fresh and accessible.
- **Plickers** (www.plickers.com): This is an effective, yet simple, tool that allows teachers to collect real-time formative assessment data without the need for pupil devices. Download the app and print yourself a set of Plicker cards. You can check pupil understanding by asking them a question. The app will read each pupil's answer according to the way in which they hold up the cards. It's absolutely brilliant for checking pupils' understanding quickly in lessons and it supports

pupils' wellbeing too, as it gives all of them a chance to participate without feeling self-conscious.

- **IPEVO visualisers**: These are just brilliant for sharing pupils' work quickly in the classroom. The wireless device connects to your screen and pupils can see exactly what work you wish to show them. Not only does this allow for quick progress in lessons, but pupil confidence is also boosted because they feel pride that their work has been chosen to be shared.

- **Vocal Recall**: This is a fairly new app that cuts marking time dramatically. It allows you to vocally record your feedback for students on the app. The app then adds your recorded feedback to QR codes that the students can scan to hear their feedback. The company sends you printable QR codes for free or you can buy them in sticker format for a small price.

- **Typorama**: This app transforms your text into beautiful typographic designs automatically. It's great for wanting to share key information with pupils and saves you lots of time making your own. You simply choose a background, type in the text and the app does the work of making beautiful typography for you.

- **The Poetry Foundation app**: If you are looking for poetry to teach, this app is brilliant. It allows you to choose a theme and then offers you all kinds of poems to explore with your pupils. It even has a randomiser tool that automatically selects poems at random, which is great for studying unseen poetry.

#technologytimesaver
#learn
#connect

Idea 31: Effective to do lists

Creating lists keeps you focused and prioritises your workload.

I don't know about you but I absolutely love writing lists. It helps me to organise my thoughts and I feel a huge sense of satisfaction when I get through the tasks I've listed as important. On the flip side of this, however, I can often feel tortured if I don't complete everything on the list. That's where the following advice can come in useful. Writing an endless list of tasks that need completing is only going to make you feel stressed and, in effect, you are setting yourself up to fail if you do this every day. The following tips are a useful way of organising your day without feeling overwhelmed with work.

1. **Plan ahead**: Write your list the night before. I read this in an article a few years ago and it's definitely made me more proactive in the mornings. With a plan already in place, you can get started straight away when you arrive at work the next day.
2. **Keep your list short**: There's no point writing a list as long as your arm if you know the likelihood is you won't complete everything. This will result in you feeling like you haven't been productive and stress will begin to seep in. Create a short list of five or fewer tasks. Think about which tasks are the most important and add them for that day.
3. **Choose your tasks carefully**: Do they really need to be on the list if they are small tasks? This will only take up space for the more important strategic tasks that need to be undertaken. Try not to avoid the difficult jobs. The wonderful Jill Berry (@jillberry102) calls this 'eating the frog'. You will feel much better once you have tackled the important but difficult tasks first.
4. **Prioritise the tasks on your list**: Ask yourself which of the tasks is the most important. Then make this your first priority.
5. **Use sticky notes**: This will help to create a more visual list and you can stick them somewhere visible.

Next steps

Buy one notepad specifically for work tasks and one for home tasks. That way you can track your progress over time and check to see if you have the balance right.

#todolists
#learn

Idea 32: Know your time

Know when you are most productive and use your time wisely.

Often, you hear people say, 'I'm such a morning person' or 'I'm a real night owl'. What they mean by these statements is that they are probably most productive when they are up early or awake late in the evenings. It makes sense then, as teachers, to figure out what time of the day we are most productive and plan accordingly.

Here are some ways you can make the most of your day by using the time that is most productive for you:

- If you know you are more productive in the morning, rise an hour earlier and get some work done before the school day starts. I'm definitely a morning person and the hour I have before the pupils arrive at school is totally precious. I get more done in that short space of time than I do for the rest of the day.
- If you are a night owl, do the same thing. Make some time each evening to plan the day or week ahead. Just make sure you get the extra sleep you need in the morning to be able to get through the day.
- Plan your tasks the day or the week before. Ensure your most difficult task is completed first. This will make you feel good, as the tough tasks will be out of the way. Plus, you will have the most energy to deal with them if you do them first.
- Avoid planning too much to do in the time you have set yourself. This can lead to feeling like you haven't achieved much when in reality you probably have!
- Find a space to work that supports your planning. For me, I use my classroom in the morning, as it's calm and quiet. If you have a space at home, make sure it is suitable for your needs. It's no good trying to plan at home if there are a number of easy distractions like the television, for example. Avoid setting yourself up to fail by creating a workspace that's right for you, and use that space during your most productive hour of the day.

#notice
#knowyourtime

Idea 33: Perfect planning

Planning effectively can save you hours of time.

As I mentioned in Idea 27, I recently set up a Twitter survey asking teachers to vote on which activity took up the most of their time. Planning and preparation came a close second to marking. As a new teacher many years ago, I remember spending hours and hours planning resources and lessons for my classes. The detail that went into my PowerPoints was incredible and I became a tiny bit obsessed with how nice it all looked. If only I had known then what I know now. Namely, that it was a ridiculous drain on my time and had very little impact, if any at all, on the progress of the pupils in my class.

Today's education system is fraught with activities that simply drain teacher time. We all need to be a little more conscious of this and one of the ways I have done this is by planning smartly. Below are some tips to help you get started on being a more efficient planner.

- **Prepare in advance**: Better to be forearmed than reactive. At the end of each year, find out what the medium- and long-term plans are for your curriculum area and prepare yourself for the term or year ahead. What resources do you need? Is there a topic you are less confident about? Do you need to read around the topic first? Do you have access to relevant reading material? Are you expected to contribute to schemes of learning? These are all questions you should be asking yourself before the new school term or year arrives.
- **Prepare for the first week back before you leave at the end of a term**: The last thing any teacher wants is to return to work after a lovely break and feel immediately panicked because they aren't fully prepared. Give yourself some time before you break up to sit and plan what needs to be done. That way, you won't feel the need to work through your precious time off and you'll have an idea of what you're doing before you arrive on that first day back.
- **Read ahead**: This point is so important. If you know you need to research a topic, make sure you give yourself enough time to do so. Before I teach a text in English, I make sure I have read the book more than once. There is also no shame in buying the study guides for the texts or topics you teach. I buy as many as I can and read

them before planning my units. The more informed you are about the topic you plan to teach, the better the teaching will be.

- **Plan collaboratively**: Great teams work well together to plan and prepare resources. I've worked in schools where everyone is working individually and planning lessons for the same topic, yet no one is sharing anything. At one school, I felt like I had started as a new teacher all over again because of the time planning took. It seems ludicrous to work in such a way. If you're part of a great team, collaborative planning will happen already. If you're not, question the way things operate. You shouldn't have to work alone when you are part of a much larger team.

- **Develop a wider network**: Building an online professional network can save you hours of time. Share and gain ideas on Twitter. You can even take part in the weekly chats to develop your subject knowledge. There are hundreds of educational Twitter chat hashtags now, such as #UKEdChat and #engchat, which you can use to keep up to date with your subject area. There is also a phenomenal bunch of teachers on Twitter who share their ideas freely. Follow hashtags such as #TeamEnglish, for example. I am in constant awe at the amount of effort and the quality of the resources people have shared in this way. I'm already indebted to some fantastic teachers who willingly (and at no cost) share their resources with the wider educational community.

- **Use online live documents**: If you can't be in the same place as your colleagues, try using online live documents to plan collaboratively. A great example is Google Drive. The work can be accessed by everyone and changes are saved as you work. It's a live document so more than one person can access it at the same time. This saves time and means everyone can be a little more efficient.

#perfectplanner
#learn
#connect

Idea 34: The 80/20 rule

Figuring out what areas of your work have the most impact will save you hours of time and improve pupil progress.

The 80/20 rule was invented by an economist named Vilfredo Pareto over a hundred years ago. He figured out that 80% of the wealth in Italy was owned by only 20% of the country's population and, weirdly, that 80% of the peas in his garden were produced by 20% of the pea plants! The rule is that 80% of any given effects come from 20% of the causes. Put into educational terms, 80% of pupil achievement results come from 20% of the work we do with our pupils.

It goes without saying then that if we figure out which of the 20% of tasks we do each day, week, term or year are most effective, we can save a heap of time. Think about your own working day. Write a list of all the things you could stop doing tomorrow, knowing that nothing would change as a result.

Here are some ideas:

- **Emails**: Stop the constant flow of emails by avoiding responding to them straight away. Deal with them once or twice a day at most. I'm pretty sure this won't affect the long-term goal of pupil achievement. For more on how to manage your inbox, see Idea 28.
- **Admin tasks**: Are they absolutely necessary? If so, do them quickly and avoid putting them off. Even better, delegate them to someone else. They have little impact on the long-term goal.
- **Lessons**: Stop making bling-style, beautiful PowerPoints. Sure, they look nice but what impact are they having on the long-term goal? Pupils will learn, whether you have an animated slide or not.
- **Marking**: Stop marking every page of work with endless annotations and pointless comments. There is much more on this in Idea 27 and Idea 82.
- **Displays**: Do them once and leave them up all year, or only make minor changes. Consider the impact they are having on the end goal (or lack of).
- **Put the phone down**: Stop checking your phone at every opportunity. You may be looking for teaching ideas on Twitter, but you are

likely to get distracted by other social media forums and messages from friends and family. Put the phone out of reach and check it once during the day, if you must. I keep mine in my bag, which sits in the staffroom.

- **Recognise the empty tasks**: Review your lesson plans and ask yourself this question: is this activity developing the pupils' learning, or is it merely a time-filler? You'll know the answer when you consider what they are learning from the process. Cut out any dead activities and focus more on the actual learning.

- **Avoid unnecessary conversations**: Some people can talk at you forever, especially if you are in a leadership role. Learn to be firm with them and your time when needed. There's a time and a place for general chit-chat, and during one of your non-contact lessons is not necessarily it. Think of the planning you could get done instead.

- **Review all meetings**: Consider whether you actually need to have a meeting. Can it be said over email? I've genuinely thought this a number of times when coming out of a meeting that took over an hour of my time. With that in mind, if the meeting is absolutely necessary, stick to rigid timings. If someone overruns, tell them to shelve the rest of their information for another time. Overrunning can cost you and everyone else in the room precious planning time.

- **Be mindful of interventions and extra revisions lessons**: If you run an intervention, make sure it is well attended. It may sound harsh but an hour's intervention with a couple of pupils may not have the same impact as an hour's planning for a class of 30 pupils. Use your time wisely. Offer an alternative for the pupils who want the extra help. Converge groups to make a bigger one if needs be.

#80/20
#learn
#notice

Next steps
Meet with the head of the school and share this theory! Make your entire school an 80/20 school. This could save staff hours, enabling them to focus on what is really important for that end goal: pupil achievement both academically and pastorally.

Idea 35: Review and reflect, so you don't forget

Keeping track of your successes each week saves time when you are planning new work.

In 2014, I started a blog on Staffrm. The aim for me was to share ideas and contribute to the wider educational community. Over time, I had gathered over 50 blog posts. I found that by writing about ideas I had used in my class, or about my reflections on teaching and wellbeing, I had collated a whole bank of knowledge to come back to whenever I pleased. Not only that, the whole process was very cathartic and ended up a useful tool when thinking about how to manage my own wellbeing. I also enjoyed comments from other educators about how my ideas had worked for them too.

The idea that we should reflect on our journey as educators is a powerful one for the reasons mentioned above, but that doesn't mean we all have to start writing a blog straight away. Why not keep a small record of your successes (and failures) in your planner or notebook? Here are a few ways to keep track:

- **Use your planner**: At the end of every day, spend five or ten minutes making a note next to each lesson plan on what worked and what didn't. It doesn't have to be much. A simple colour-coding system where you highlight the best bits of the lesson would suffice. This seems manageable to me and is something I do when I don't feel I have the time to blog. You'll have an entire year's worth of reflections to use come the end of the school year, which may be useful for the following one. Obviously, you can return to your reflections much sooner than that if you need to. If daily reflections seem like a big stretch for you, why not do it weekly and see how you get on?
- **Folder filing**: Create a folder on your computer and fill it with really successful lessons. Simply drop them in at the end of the day or week. When you are really struggling for time or just can't think of an idea for a lesson, return to your folder and use something you know works well. Better still, have a shared folder that your teaching buddies can contribute to and use as well.

- **Sticky notes on a shared board**: In our department workroom, we have a 'what went well' board. Staff can jot down their successes on a sticky note and add it on the board for everyone else to see (and use). It works well because, let's face it, teachers love to talk about their lessons! It's also really quick and it feels fun sharing. The board is cleared each term to make way for new, fresh teaching ideas. What I like about this is that it's constantly changing as we teach. It never remains stagnant, making way for innovative pedagogy as well as old favourites. It's also great because everyone contributes, which encourages greater collaboration.
- **Start your own blog**: When you are ready, why not begin writing your own reflective blog? If you feel like it's a big leap in the dark, begin by reading other blogs. Find out what interests you and then think about what type of blog you would like to write. I guarantee, your ideas will be worth sharing if you're feeling brave enough. On the other hand, if it's a reflective piece you have written and you just can't bring yourself to press that send button, store it for your own personal use or share it with friends first to get some initial feedback. It took me a while to share my own first piece, but once you've made the leap, it gets much easier. It's also a great feeling knowing that what you have written is helping other educators out there. I highly recommend Staffrm as a first-time blogging spot. It's very user-friendly; even the worst technophobes will be able to navigate its pages. Another good thing to mention is that it has a 500-word limit, which I found really helpful for a number of reasons. Firstly, it stopped me waffling on too much and helped me keep my ideas clear and succinct for readers. Secondly, it saved me time, as it doesn't take long at all to write a 500-word piece. There are also heaps of other blogs on there for you to access once you have an account.

#reviewandreflect
#learn
#connect

Next steps

Why not create your own blog on the web? Once you have built up enough courage to begin sharing, it seems an obvious next step to have your own blog space where all your best ideas and reflections are stored. I'd love to hear about your blogging journey once you get started.

Idea 36: Work blocks

Organising your work into blocks or episodes ensures you are more productive with each task.

We all love half term for obvious reasons; it gives us a chance to recharge, visit family and friends or even see a bit of the world. However, it's also one of those weird breaks where you usually still have some work to do and it always feels as though there isn't enough time to do it. During half term, it's so easy, and necessary for some, to lose routine and it can be difficult to find the motivation to work. The week usually flies by and you can find yourself doing very little in terms of work, which is great if you want to down tools completely, but not if you do have some work to get through. It can be all too easy to find yourself frantically working the Sunday evening hours away to get it all done, which isn't ideal for anyone.

One way to manage this is by moving and working in blocks. The idea is that you plan your day to take place in blocks and decide what you would like to get done in each block. This works best when you complete the blocks in different locations. For example, one day you could plan to go to work and tidy the office, before moving to your classroom to plan some assessments, and then heading out to a coffee shop to complete some marking. You don't move on to each new location until you have completed the tasks you set out to do.

The important thing to remember is to keep your tasks realistic and take breaks in between each block. A short walk, cycle or drive to your next destination provides the break your brain needs before you get started again. An added benefit is that it keeps you quite active as you move from place to place, and you may even get to explore some new places you wouldn't necessarily have done had you not planned your day in blocks. Why not give it a try next half term and see how you get on?

To really up the challenge, add time constraints to your block work. This supports a theory called 'Parkinson's Law' whereby 'work expands so as to fill the time available for its completion'. We've all been there: you had a year to write your assignment yet you squeezed it into the last week of summer. You had reports to write and were given the month but you chose to do them at the very last minute, potentially using your weekend to get them done. Why? Because people work to deadlines and if there's plenty of time available, why rush? This actually results in less productivity, but if you use Parkinson's Law to your advantage, you can eliminate this. Add it to your work block planning and you may well get a lot more done in the time you have allowed for yourself.

Here are some tips for using this theory:

- Work without your laptop charger and race against the battery power. It will force you to get more done.
- Restrict your time throughout the day and only plan a few blocks instead of many.
- Only plan work blocks for when you are most productive. So if you know you get more done in the morning, avoid too many blocks in the afternoon. The same goes for any night owls; plan your blocks in the evening and get some extra sleep in the morning.
- Tell someone what time you intend to finish work, and if you run over, force them to give you a forfeit. I often do this and it works wonders, as I never want to get the first round in!
- Set a hard deadline; you'll be amazed at how well you stick to it.
- Only work during coffee shop hours. Set your deadline for closing time and you will be forced to work more quickly. Better still, arrive a couple of hours before closing time and work within that tighter time frame.
- Allow yourself treats or rewards when you complete each block. A chocolate bar usually does the trick for me, but for bigger tasks, why not treat yourself to a night out once it is complete? It will make you work more productively to get the tasks done.

#workblocks
#learn
#notice

Idea 37: Data demon

Knowing the difference between useless data and useful data is important.

Data is a topical debate between teachers. It has played a large role in schools in recent years due to schools looking to measure just about anything and everything in their control (the Ofsted effect). However, not all data is useful at all times and it's important to be able to distinguish between dud data and useful data that will support the learning journey of your pupils.

A good starting point would be to remember that good data starts and ends with the pupil, a point raised by a wonderful maths teacher by the name of Rebecca Skarshewski (@bec_skar). She delivered a brilliant training session to the NQTs on my course and she has very kindly allowed me to share the following information from the session with you here.

It is important to note that data comes in all forms: quizzing, Pupil Premium information, special educational needs information, data from previous schools, reading scores, gender data, test results, formative and summative assessments, and the list goes on. The question is, how do we know which data is useful and when? The answer to this question depends upon why you are collecting the data in the first place. For example, is it to check attainment progress or is it to plan for your next lesson? By making sure your data is all of the following, you can be sure to avoid wasting time with unnecessary data whilst also improving the progress of your pupils.

- **Collected for a purpose**: This will inform your planning from the start. Why are you collecting the data? Is it to report to parents? Is it to assess progress on a unit of work? Consider this first before you take action, and make a record of what you will need to do.
- **Quantitative**: Unless data is quantifiable, it will be very difficult to measure. Make sure that your data is quantified and you are on the right track.
- **Concise**: Data must be concise in order to avoid too much confusion about what is being measured. Your data must be brief but comprehensive. This makes it much clearer to see progress or lack of.

- **Contextual**: If data isn't contextual, it can be useless. Knowing that someone can't swim, for example, isn't useful data for a maths lesson. It goes without saying, then, that not all data is useful all of the time. It is important to know which data is important and when.
- **Rigorous and robust**: Data collection must be planned in advance and a strict pattern or procedure must be agreed. Otherwise, you may find it difficult to measure in the long run, as irregular data collection compromises outcomes.
- **Used to deliver next steps**: Great data will show you what you intended it to show you. If you planned your data collection carefully, you will be able to see useful information in the data. For example, if you assessed pupils on a unit of work, you should be able to see which skills pupils have successfully mastered and which they need some more practice with. Use the data wisely to plan your next steps.

Here's a simple model to follow:

1. Start with a question – what are you trying to determine about your pupils' learning?
2. Develop a test that is fair and relevant – does it comprehensively test all the content required? Does it give you the information you need?
3. Ensure the validity of your data – are your results repeatable? Have you made any assumptions that will affect your data?
4. Apply the results to teaching practice – this could include re-teaching topics, targeted intervention, targeted support from teaching assistants, differentiation in class and altered seating arrangements, to name but a few.

Next steps

Data collated by yourself is useful for your own classes but what about your whole department, key stage or school? Does your school use shared data trackers and ask all teachers to input their data after each assessment point? If not, why not suggest it? It's a useful tool to look at whole-cohort performance.

#datademon
#learn

Idea 38: What's the point of lesson objectives?

Telling pupils what they are going to learn is far quicker than writing it down everywhere and asking pupils to do the same.

As a trainee teacher, I was told that lesson objectives were important. They informed planning, gave your lesson direction and helped pupils to understand what they were doing. I made sure every lesson plan had lesson objectives linked to assessment for learning aims and agonised over them if they didn't exactly match. One school I worked at insisted that all staff used the 'All, most, some' model in every lesson. In every classroom, there were teachers dutifully reciting objectives and pupils monotonously reciting them back (and I'm unconvinced they even knew what they meant). The glaringly obvious problems with this are that it implies some pupils won't be able to do the work because it is out of their reach and it offers the savvier pupils a choice as to how much of the lesson they want to take part in.

I stopped writing lesson objectives on the board over two years ago. The reason? They are a total waste of time. What does it matter if the pupils don't have them written in their books or they aren't on the board? If you want pupils to know what they're doing that lesson, just tell them and save yourself heaps of time in doing so. I'm not for one minute suggesting that you don't plan your lessons. Every lesson should be carefully thought out and part of a much bigger picture. One way that you could introduce lessons to pupils is by presenting them with 'the big question'. This big question remains throughout the scheme of work and each week, or lesson, the skill focus changes. As the weeks go on, the pupils begin to understand why each skill is so important to the bigger picture. No tedious lesson objectives needed to understand that.

#nomoreobjectives
#learn

Idea 39: Nature nurture

Spending time in nature will make you more productive in the long run.

I recently moved to London and took up a new position as Head of Department. It goes without saying that the initial pressure of the job and the move was pretty intense. I'm a country girl at heart. I grew up in a tiny village in the Vale of Belvoir that consisted of one main street, and the local shop was essentially someone's back room. There was no bus route so to go anywhere, you would have to walk, cycle or drive. The thing I miss most is the silence. The pure serenity of hearing nothing at all.

I doubt very much that I will ever get used to the constant noise of the capital, even if I do love the excitement of the place. I find myself craving nature during my busiest times and I find a wander in the park is just what I need to nurture and clear my mind. This is enough to tell me how powerful nature is for my productivity and wellbeing, but here are a few more reasons why you may need it too:

- It improves your short-term memory. Studies show that a walk in the park or through a field is better for short-term memory than a walk along a busy street. This is because your brain still has to think about a lot when you are walking in a built-up area. It makes sense to find somewhere altogether more peaceful.
- Your mental energy is boosted. A walk in nature can energise your mind and prepare you for another stint of work.
- It's a known stress-reliever. Studies show that people who relax in nature have less cortisol (a hormone related to stress) in their bodies.
- It improves your concentration. Many studies have proven this fact. Some even go so far as to suggest that just looking at images of nature has a positive effect on your concentration.
- Nature can improve your creativity. Studies have shown this to be true. So if you're at a dead end with your lesson planning, take a break in nature and come back to it.

Next steps

Why not organise a nature trip with your colleagues once a term? This will ensure that everyone benefits from nature and will also encourage greater communication.

#naturenurture
#connect
#exercise

Chapter 4

Rocking teaching and learning

Improving your teaching and learning will have a great impact on your own wellbeing and that of your pupils too.

Teaching and learning are at the heart of what makes a good teacher. Over the years, I've seen brilliant NQTs work their magic with pupils. Their enthusiasm and hard work really pay off by the end of the year and results day. Sometimes, however, I have seen it end there. After perhaps three or four years, some teachers seem to plateau; unwillingness to change, repeated lessons without development and tardy classrooms are all evidence of a teacher who is stuck in a rut. By contrast, the best teachers I know are continuously developing their subject knowledge and honing their teaching and learning skills. I believe, as teachers, we never stop learning. Anecdotally, I know I am a far better teacher now than when I first gained my QTS. That's down to my own drive to keep up to date with the constant shifting of all things educational. This chapter offers advice and guidance on how to develop your own teaching and learning, so that you feel like your teaching is constantly improving and that you are making a difference to the pupils you teach. Confidence as a teacher, brought about by honing your teaching skills and achieving excellent results for your pupils, has a direct impact on your wellbeing. Knowing that you are really making a difference to their lives makes you feel good. I hope you enjoy learning something new when you take a proactive approach to teaching and learning.

Idea 40: Own your own CPD

Taking control of your own professional development will build your skills and confidence.

Before the start of a new academic year, plan your own CPD and decide how you want to develop professionally. This can give you a real focus for the year and make you feel empowered and happier in general.

What are the options?

Get booked onto a paid course. There are plenty of courses to choose from, and if you make a booking at the beginning of the year, you are less likely to get carried away in the day-to-day routine of teaching. Meet early with your line manager to lay out your plans and make sure they are aware of how you wish to progress. That way, you will be supported by your school, and any goals you have may tie into your performance management targets.

Paid courses not a possibility? Fear not! There are plenty of free courses and opportunities to develop professionally. Universities and other education providers are offering more free courses than ever before. Search online and sign up to develop your practice for free.

TeachMeets are another great form of CPD. They stem from Edinburgh, where a group of teachers met informally in a local pub in 2006 to share ideas. Since then, they have spread worldwide. At TeachMeets there is no agenda; it's just teachers sharing their classroom practice with other teachers. You sign up to share an idea by presenting for two to seven minutes, or just go along to get some ideas for your own classroom.

#ownyourownCPD
#connect
#learn

Next steps

Research books that can support your professional development. For example, the *100 Ideas* series published by Bloomsbury Education is really useful, in particular Ross Morrison McGill's *100 Ideas for Secondary Teachers: Outstanding Lessons*. Daisy Christodoulou's *Making Good Progress?* (Oxford University Press) was also extremely helpful to me in the midst of life after levels learning.

Idea 41: Teaching and learning breakfast

Being well fed and talking about great teaching ideas really sets you up for the day.

When people come together to eat, they bond. Sharing mealtimes together is clearly important; we do it as families every day. Why not incorporate this culture into our schools and use it to develop our teaching?

This idea came from a school where I previously worked. It is really quite simple but very effective. One morning every week, staff meet to enjoy breakfast together whilst also sharing their best teaching and learning ideas. There are different ways in which this can be orchestrated. One model would be to ask staff to sign up to share their ideas on rotation, so that every week a different staff member is able to talk about what works for them. This idea works best if it is based on an informal drop-in approach. That way, you never know who is going to turn up and it's different every week.

There are many benefits to this kind of activity. Firstly, new, innovative teaching ideas are shared and classroom practice is improved. Secondly, staff not only build a plethora of ideas but also feel valued as part of the team. It's a real confidence boost to have your idea used in someone else's classroom. Thirdly, it feels great to share your ideas with other professionals. That warm feeling you get when you help others is definitely a benefit. Lastly, stronger bonds are made between staff who rarely interact with each other. If you open it up to everyone, you will have a real mix of people, from teaching staff to support staff. It's a great way to build better links between cross sections of the school and everyone feels as though they have a voice to be heard.

Next steps
Why not build on this activity and encourage staff to share their teaching and learning ideas with a wider audience? Include a slot during whole-staff briefing to ensure ideas reach every classroom.

#breakfastlearner
#volunteer
#connect
#learn

Idea 42: Speedy lesson planning

Understanding the basic elements of a lesson and sticking to them will keep things simple and save you time in the long run.

As a new teacher, I often spent hours planning lessons that were full of gimmicks and excitement. Sometimes, this resulted in the loss of the learning journey or the actual point of the lesson. Being reflective, I would ask myself, 'Did they actually learn about what I wanted them to?' and 'Could they have made better progress if I hadn't included X, Y or Z?' The answer was often that I could have helped them make progress more quickly if I had kept things simple. Below is a lesson-planning structure I now stick to in order to maximise learning in the classroom.

Connect the learning

This is all about helping the pupils draw connections between their prior knowledge and what you are about to teach them. It can be as simple as a question on the board when they arrive, or a more detailed discussion to gauge prior understanding. It can be images that connect two ideas, or even an activity that draws two topics or points together.

New information

This is the introduction of new content that you want the pupils to learn about. How you present this information is up to you. Some teachers like pupils to play an active, discovery-type role in this stage of a lesson, but I personally believe it is far more productive to just deliver this new knowledge to them. There's nothing wrong with standing at the front of a class, as the expert in the room, and teaching pupils difficult or challenging content. Don't be fooled into thinking dictatorial teaching doesn't work. It does.

Searching for meaning

Pupils get to grips with the new information here. I tend to plan an activity that requires pupils to think about the new knowledge and apply a particular skill at the same time. Modelling the process you want the pupils to go through is important here. This part of the lesson may involve pupils working together.

Demonstrating understanding

Here, the pupils put into practice their new knowledge and the skills they have been developing. For me, this part of the lesson is usually where pupils work independently from one another, demonstrating what they have learned.

Review and reflect

Finally, pupils should review their work at the end of the lesson. This can be done through self-assessment, peer-assessment or teacher instruction. It involves pupils measuring their progress and understanding what to do next.

Homework

Some teachers like to set homework at the beginning of a lesson. I prefer to get straight on with the tasks and set homework at the end. Homework should build on the knowledge pupils have acquired in the lesson or prepare them for the following few lessons.

If you stick to this format for all your lessons, you will find lesson planning becomes much easier and quicker over time.

#speedylessonplanner
#planning
#learn

Idea 43: Know your subject

Reading about your specialist subject hugely improves your teaching practice.

The idea that you finish studying once you leave university or complete your teacher training course is ludicrous. Over the years, I have seen many teachers do this exact thing. This has, in some cases, resulted in stagnant teaching and poor exam results, as the curriculum changes frequently. In my opinion, the best teachers are those who constantly aim to improve their subject knowledge. Not only do your pupils benefit greatly from this, but you also gain more confidence and a greater understanding about the subject you specialise in. Why any teacher would not want to continue to develop is unfathomable to me. Here are some ways in which you can develop your subject knowledge:

1. **Read academic books or online journal articles about your subject.** There are many of these around and they shouldn't take you too long to get through. You will be surprised at how often you refer to them in your teaching and shouldn't be fooled into thinking they are only for those officially studying.
2. **Read books that link to your subject.** They don't necessarily have to be academic in nature. For example, autobiographies of figures of interest in your field may be of use.
3. **Look for events that support an understanding of your subject.** Science shows, literature festivals and sporting events are all places where you can develop your subject knowledge.
4. **Attend subject-specific conferences.** These are common and can really add value to your understanding of all things related to your subject. You can find information about them through TES or any education supplement in the newspapers.
5. **Attend research-based conferences about your subject.** Some of the best teachers I know are those that understand why and how their subject should be taught. Their teaching is based on evidential research that has been proven to work. Again, these can be found by looking on the usual educational forums.

#subjectexpert
#learn

Idea 44: Marginal gains

Making small changes to your teaching and learning will show the best results over time.

Often, the amount of information available about teaching and learning can feel completely overwhelming to busy teachers trying to get through their working week. Not only that, teaching and learning advice and information seem to change as often as the weather. As a new teacher, I remember trying to include gimmicks galore in my lessons. I knew about every new teaching trend before most in my school and I felt like I was really clued up. When I look back at those first few years, I realise how utterly exhausting it was, not to mention how frantic it must have been for my pupils every time I tried something new. Thankfully, my teaching has changed quite a bit since then. Marginal gains go some way to preventing the kind of frantic teaching I used to display.

Marginal gains is a theory that the British cycling team put into practice in order to win the Tour de France. The idea is that small, less noticeable changes have more impact on your life than those more memorable, bigger changes that you give far too much credit to. It is the one per cent margin of everything you do. The fact is that every significant change in your life is the result of much smaller decisions. If this theory is applied to teaching, over time, you are much more likely to notice the small, but consistent, changes you make to your teaching, rather than trying to make too many changes all at once. The latter often leads to rejection of such changes and a feeling of failure for the teacher.

To avoid overworking yourself and trying to change too many things at once, why not apply marginal gains to your teaching? What one area could you change by one per cent? Try one new idea or change one way you do something each half term. That way you are giving yourself time to build the new idea or change it into a habit. Once the habit is established, you can change one more thing and so on. By the end of the academic year, you should see a remarkable difference in your teaching and the pupils' progress, and you will have improved or made changes to your teaching six times without feeling too overwhelmed.

#changeonething
#learn

Idea 45: Attend or deliver a TeachMeet

TeachMeets are informal gatherings with all things teaching and learning at the heart of them.

As I mentioned in Idea 40, TeachMeets began in 2006 in Edinburgh, Scotland. Teachers were looking for ways in which to connect with other like-minded professionals and share ideas on a wider scale. If you haven't attended a TeachMeet yet, I strongly recommend them to you. Essentially, they are informal gatherings where teachers share ideas that have worked in their classroom. They are a great way to develop your classroom practice as well as make new connections.

Tickets are usually free and you can go along as a participant without presenting. If you're feeling particularly brave, however, you can sign up to present an idea of your own. There are a few different formats for TeachMeets now, but the most common types of presentation are:

- micro-presentations, which last up to seven minutes (the original reason for this was that it takes seven minutes to drink a pint, hence the informal nature of the events!)
- nano-presentations, which are just two minutes long
- break-out tables, where ideas are shared to a smaller audience on rotation.

With the variety on offer, it is easy to find a TeachMeet that suits your style.

My best advice to those who wish to attend a TeachMeet for the first time is to try not to become overwhelmed with all the ideas shared. It would be impossible to try everything. I always take away one idea and try that for half a term, before moving on to something else. Remember, what works for one teacher may not necessarily work for you.

Once you have attended a few TeachMeets, why not be brave and plan and deliver your own? The following steps will help you during the planning stages:

1. Decide on the type of TeachMeet you would like to run. Will it have a specific focus such as English, for example? Or will it be open to everyone on a more general scale?

2. Decide on a venue and a date. I would recommend planning a TeachMeet to take place at least six months from the initial planning stages, as this will give you plenty of time to promote the event and gather speakers.
3. Get yourself some keynote speakers. These will add some sparkle to your event and make sure your tickets are booked.
4. Gather sponsors and prizes. There are many education-based businesses that will be more than willing to support your event. A TeachMeet would not be the same without a Twinkl mug and an IPEVO visualiser! Bloomsbury also love to sponsor TeachMeets.
5. Create an eye-catching infographic to promote your event on Twitter.
6. Set up your event on Eventbrite. This way you can track how many tickets have been sold and inform delegates of any changes in one swift email.
7. Set up the details of your TeachMeet on the official front page (http://teachmeet.pbworks.com/w/page/19975349/FrontPage) and link to your ticket page on Eventbrite. That way people can easily follow the link to make a booking.
8. Promote, promote, promote! This is crucial. If no one knows about the event, it will be a pretty small turnout. Share the event on Twitter daily. Use local links too. Newspapers, consortium emails and word of mouth will get your event noticed.
9. If you struggle to get presenters, ask people. You will be surprised at how many teachers say yes to such requests!
10. Make sure you have a host to take delegates through the event smoothly. Choose them wisely. They will need to be able to hold a crowd of potentially very tired but enthusiastic educators.
11. Organise food and drink for the event well in advance. This is another reason ticket numbers are useful.
12. Ensure you have helpers at the event to direct delegates and make sure everything goes smoothly in terms of logistics.
13. Have fun! Remember, the idea behind TeachMeets is that they are informal gatherings where current classroom practitioners share ideas with a friendly crowd.

#teachmeets
#learn
#connect

Idea 46: Observation expert

Observing other teachers in action is hugely valuable for your own teaching practice.

We are forever telling our pupils that they learn from each other so why not practise what we preach? Over the academic year, decide on a number of observations you would like to undertake based on your own personal targets, and go and see other teachers in action. Here are some areas to consider:

Observation aim	Who to observe
Understanding of a particular special educational need	Observe the SENDCo Shadow a pupil for the day Shadow a teaching assistant for the day
Literacy or numeracy	Observe an English or maths teacher Observe the literacy or numeracy coordinator in a lesson Attend a literacy or numeracy meeting
Subject knowledge	Observe your faculty leader Observe a higher key stage lesson
Planning and delivery	Observe a teaching and learning leader
Assessment for learning	Visit the exams team Observe a lead teacher
Differentiation	Observe a mixed-ability class Observe the SENDCo with small groups

Aim for one observation every half term and have a specific idea of what you would like to see. By the end of the year, you should feel more confident in the area you wanted to work on.

Next steps

Be brave! Ask someone to observe you at the start of the year and then again once you have observed others to see the progress you've made.

#observerexpert
#connect
#learn

Idea 47: Inspiration spy

Being on the lookout for teaching inspiration and ideas saves you time.

This idea can be split into two areas: useful teaching items and useful teaching ideas. I'll deal with them both in turn.

Teaching items

I am what can only be described as a magpie when it comes to inspiration for teaching. If I see something I think might be useful (and it's free or relatively cheap), I'll take it. I have come to acquire a large collection of things that have really engaged pupils with certain topics. I have some shrapnel from the Somme Battlefields that I show pupils when we are studying war poetry. I was told by a tour guide that it was armoured communication wire. It really brought everything home to me when I was on the tour and it now affords my pupils the same connection with the event. I also have an authentic Texas cowboy hat, which I have out when I'm teaching *Of Mice and Men*. My cupboards are full of leaflets, travel brochures and maps, all of which add value to my lessons. These are all items I collected whilst going about my everyday life. It took no extra time to get them. What items have you come across that could add that something extra to your lessons?

Teaching ideas

A fantastic primary teacher by the name of Stephen Lockyer reminded me of this at a recent TeachMeet. He believes that as teachers, we should read around our specialist areas and look for teaching inspiration in other, not so obvious, places. I wholeheartedly agree. The example he gave was about Wagamama and the way they design their restaurants. Their tables are at right angles to their serving area so that the food can be served to customers in the shortest amount of time possible. Stephen used this simple, yet effective, idea to change the way he organised his classroom so that he could easily and quickly access each of his pupils. This is just one example of how teaching inspiration can come from areas outside of education. Be on the lookout at all times!

#inspirationspy
#connect
#learn

Idea 48: Make time for TED Talks

TED Talks provide inspiration and discussion around education and may just get you thinking differently about your own teaching.

If you don't know what TED Talks are by now, then you're in for a treat! TED is a non-profit organisation devoted to spreading ideas in the form of short videos. It began in 1984 as a conference about technology, entertainment and design and, since then, it has grown in popularity to the extent that it now covers every topic imaginable, including education. Its mission is to spread ideas and develop a deeper understanding of the world. It believes that ideas have the power to change people's attitudes, lives and, eventually, the world.

As you can imagine, over the years there have been many TED Talks about education. Some of the most popular talks are listed here:

- For inspiration about the teaching profession, watch 'Every Kid Needs a Champion' by Rita Pierson. This talk is inspiring and heartfelt, and it provides a poignant reminder of the power of education.
- For ideas about resilience, watch 'Grit: The Power of Passion and Perseverance' by Angela Lee Duckworth. This talk gives a fascinating insight into the power of never giving up.
- For ideas about making progress, watch 'The Power of Believing That You Can Improve' by Carol Dweck. Dweck is famous for her research into what is now called 'growth mindset'. Here she explores the power of believing in yourself.
- For debate about creativity in schools, watch 'Do Schools Kill Creativity?' by Sir Ken Robinson. Robinson has sparked controversial debate with his ideas but, whatever side of the fence you sit on, this is worth a watch.

Next steps

Do you have a passion for a particular area of education? Why not deliver your own TED Talk? There are many independent TEDx Talks around the country that you can apply to. Be brave and give it a go!

#TEDTalks
#connect
#learn

Idea 49: Pedagogy wheel

Knowing the ingredients of a great lesson will save you time and ensure your lessons are consistently effective.

This idea is similar to Idea 42 in that it provides you with ideas to support great lesson planning. Whilst 'Speedy lesson planning' is about the learning journey of a lesson, 'Pedagogy wheel' can be helpful when deciding what to include in a lesson.

The idea came from a wonderful colleague of mine, Claire Thompson. Originally, she came up with six key areas of teaching and learning that should be seen in a lesson. From that, she created the pedagogy wheel (which is essentially like a pie chart!), which contains activities you could try in your lessons in order to achieve all six areas.

Here are the six topics and ideas you could use in your lesson:

Literacy
Literacy is key to planning lessons and every teacher should ensure that the pupils in their class are receiving the support they need to access their subject content. This can be done in a number of ways. Some examples include: writing frames, keyword glossaries, sentence starters, conjunction boards, directed activities related to texts, features of text checklists, thought stems, slow writing and many more.

Active learning
It can be easy to fall into the trap of thinking that active learning means all pupils should be up and out of their seat taking part in various activities, but it isn't always the case. In fact, active learning means 'pupils participate in the process and they participate when they are doing something besides passively listening' (Charles Bonwell and James Eison, *Active Learning: Creating Excitement in the Classroom*, Jossey-Bass, 1991). It's worth noting that there's nothing wrong with pupils listening to a teacher delivering new content and explaining difficult concepts. In fact, it's often the quickest way for the expert in the room to impart knowledge, but at some point pupils will need to do something with that information and think about what they are doing too. That's where

active learning plays a role. Activities you could try include: 'think, pair, share', carousel activities, structured group work, walking or talking mocks, metacognition tasks, extract analysis, sorting activities, role-playing, peer teaching, debates, presentations and class discussion.

Differentiation

Differentiation is the action or process of differentiating or distinguishing between two or more things or people. In education, that means being aware of the needs of our pupils and incorporating them into our planning, so that all pupils have the best possible chance of learning. This falls into three areas: readiness to learn, learning needs and interest. These needs can be catered for in a number of ways, including by task, grouping, resources, pace, outcome, dialogue and assessment. Let's look at each of these in turn.

- **Task**: This can mean different worksheets for different pupils in the same class (personally, I think there is little time for this). Another way of differentiating by task would be to have one resource that gets progressively more difficult.
- **Grouping**: Seating plans can be used to differentiate, as can paired groupings or structured group work.
- **Resources**: Not all pupils will be able to access advanced resources that you may wish to introduce to your pupils. A variety of resources may be needed, varying from texts at a basic level with illustrations to those using more advanced vocabulary and complex ideas.
- **Pace**: This can be tricky when you have pupils working through tasks at different speeds. Extension tasks are helpful here, as well as using available resources such as teaching assistants to support the pupils moving at a slower pace.
- **Outcome**: This is the acceptance that pupils will reach a different outcome based on the same activity being taught. It takes the least time to prepare but runs the risk that some pupils may fall below the standard that is expected upon completion of the task.
- **Dialogue**: This is where the skill of the teacher plays a big role. Teachers use targeted questioning to develop pupils' understanding of a topic. They change the way they explain things to support the needs of the pupils in their class.
- **Assessment**: This takes place in the classroom in an ongoing fashion to check the understanding of the pupils in the class and adjust the learning journey accordingly.

Assessment for learning

This is the idea that teachers check the progress of their pupils regularly to ensure they are making progress. It can be done in a number of ways: mini quizzes, self- or peer-assessment, using mini whiteboards, exit cards, highlighting success criteria, success checklists, RAG-rated success criteria and so on.

Modelling

This should take place frequently. If we expect pupils to complete something to a high standard, we must show them what that standard looks like. Likewise, modelling good practice is also helpful. Examples include: teacher-made examples, live marking, exam board exemplars, walking or talking mocks, using visualisers to share excellent pupil examples, the teacher modelling tasks such as reading and using pupils to model good practice.

Targeted questioning

This is another form of differentiation that, when done well, can really develop pupils' understanding of a topic you are teaching. The idea behind this is to get the pupils thinking about things at a deeper level. It may involve thinking critically or in an evaluative way. Some ways this can be done are: using 'pose-pause-pounce-bounce', asking specific pupils questions, asking pupils to choose another pupil to add to their response or answer the next question, using Bloom's taxonomy to structure your questions and probing pupils' responses with 'how' and 'why' questions.

#pedagogywheel
#connect
#learn
#notice

Idea 50: Know your pupils

Understanding the needs of your pupils is a must for developing their progress.

I have always believed that relationships are the key to successful schools and still stand by that statement today. One of the most important aspects of teaching and learning is getting to know your pupils. Firstly, if pupils see we are taking the time to get to know them, they will become more invested in school. Building these relationships early on is vital. Secondly, we need to create a learning environment in which pupils feel able to progress. Knowing them will support this aim. Finally, and rather importantly, if we don't know our pupils, how can we possibly plan their learning activities effectively? We need to know about their needs before we can successfully support them to make progress. Below are just a few ways you can get to know your pupils better and strengthen your relationships with them.

- **Learn their names.** Aim to do this in the first week or two. I realise that this is quite difficult if you only see a class once every week! Use name tags if you need to and always say their name when you are talking to them. It'll help you remember them more quickly.
- **Create a pupil survey.** Ask your pupils about their likes, dislikes and so on, so you can get to know them more quickly. Try 'I wish my teacher knew...' as a sentence starter. A teacher called Kyle Schwartz in the US did this with her class and ended up with some heartbreaking results, but it is useful to see their responses and know what they are dealing with. See this link for more details: http://iwishmyteacherknewbook.com.
- **Collect and display birthdays.** This is a particularly nice thing to do as a form tutor. You can even put birthday bunting up over your form board. Pupils love it when everyone at school celebrates their birthday with them.
- **Get to know their families.** This really does help to build relationships and support you as a teacher in the long run. Make a point of trying to talk to all your pupils' parents before the end of the first half term. Keeping regular communication with parents can really support your pupils' learning.
- **Use their data.** You will (or should) have been given data for each of your pupils, whether that be the previous year's information or

SATs results, or other information like whether the child has SEN status, is on free school meals or is a pupil who qualifies for Pupil Premium funding. Use this information wisely to inform your planning and teaching.

- **Make sure you know them all.** My current headteacher talks about RHINOs – pupils who are 'really here in name only'. They are the pupils who pass through the school day rarely being spoken to. Make sure this doesn't happen with your pupils by talking to them all individually.

#knowyourpupils
#connect
#learn

Idea 51: Literacy legend

Literacy is vital to ensuring pupils make progress in your lesson.

Literacy is split into three main areas: oracy, reading and writing. The following are just a few ideas you can use to develop the literacy skills of your pupils.

Oracy

- Use thought stems (an idea originally coined by David Didau) to show pupils how to begin a sentence. Examples would be 'The author has tried to…' or 'The word X is interesting because…'. I have these on my board at the front of my classroom to support pupils.
- Ask pupils to repeat spoken phrases formally, as if they were writing their response on paper. This encourages them to use the language you want to see in their writing. For example, if a pupil responds to a question with 'because she can't bear to live without him', ask them to formally rephrase the sentence to 'Juliet is acting irrationally because she can't bear the thought of living without Romeo'.
- Ask pupils to use keywords in their oral responses. This will help them to contextualise the words and understand them better.
- Don't accept 'I don't know' as a response. Tell pupils you will come back to them in a couple of minutes after they have thought about it.

Reading

- Teach pupils to skim and scan for relevant information by looking for keywords in the text. This is different to reading everything on the page and is a valuable skill for them to learn.
- Ask and expect pupils to read aloud. This will develop their understanding of the text and their reading skills.
- Model how to annotate a written piece. Visualisers are brilliant for this. Talk pupils through the process as you go. This metacognitive activity has achieved excellent results for me.

Writing

- Use sentence starters and writing frames to support pupils with writing.
- Model. Show pupils what a finished writing piece looks like. They need to see it before they begin their own.

- Use 'slow writing' (another David Didau idea). Slow writing is where the teacher directly instructs pupils on what to write for each sentence. For example, sentence one is a topic sentence, sentence two is a rhetorical question, sentence three is a one-word sentence, and so on. It supports pupils' understanding of writing structure and impact of writing.
- Use structure strips. An idea originally thought up by Stephen Lockyer, structure strips are bookmark in size and, like slow writing, they instruct pupils on what to write in each section of their response. They are essentially a step-by-step set of instructions for each stage of writing. For example, the first instruction might be 'Introduce the topic' and the second might be 'Write a topic sentence to begin you paragraph' and so on. If all instructions are followed, the end result is an effective piece of writing. This idea has been a complete hit on Twitter, with many teachers sharing their resources for free. They are also very pretty and colourful, and who doesn't like colourful resources?

#literacylegend
#learn

Idea 52: Tidy targets

Setting yourself targets for the year will ensure you stay on track and work on areas that you have chosen to develop.

Target setting has been helping people to achieve their goals for years. These days in education, your performance management meetings usually involve some sort of target-setting activity. Before this takes place, it can be a good idea to think about what you want to achieve over the year and what skills or knowledge you want to develop. Otherwise, you can feel as though you are just existing day to day without any real development. That's when teaching can become stagnant, which is something we all need to avoid. I have been using SMART targets for a few years now; they have definitely helped me stay on track with my goals.

SMART targets are specific, measurable, achievable, realistic and time-bound. A specific target is something that is perfectly clear to everyone who views it. It is unambiguous. Measurable means that it can be broken down into steps that can also be measured. Obviously, the clearer the target, the easier it is to measure. An achievable target is one that can be achieved with the resources and time that you have available to you. There is no point setting a grandiose target that you simply cannot achieve for whatever reason. The same goes for realistic targets. Choose a target you are confident you can achieve. Lastly, time-bound targets give you a time frame to work within. These targets can then be broken down over the year to keep you on track.

At the start of the year, set yourself SMART targets that you want to have achieved by the end of the academic year. Once these are decided, you can plan how you aim to get there over the six half terms. Ask yourself the following questions: what do I want to have achieved by the end of the first half term? And the second? And so on. This will help you to achieve the overall targets for the year and give you a sense of purpose as you plan.

#tidytargets
#learn

Chapter 5
Supporting pupils

If pupil wellbeing is taken care of, they are more likely to succeed.

I'm a firm believer in making pupils' education in the classroom an enjoyable one. Building positive relationships is a large part of the process of teaching and expecting students to achieve. The teachers I remember the most from my own school days weren't the ones who came in, taught and then left every day. They were the teachers who took the time to ask me about my learning, to ask me how my day was going, to care about me as a person. Building relationships is important because teaching is often a difficult profession, not least because pupils themselves don't always want to learn. In some schools, low-level disruption can be dealt with swiftly and effectively, which means you can get on with the job you chose to do: teach. However, I have worked in schools where this isn't the case. Low-level disruption was rife and part and parcel of daily routine if you didn't have a handle on your classes. It was under those circumstances I tried a variety of ideas to hook pupils in and expect learning. Some of the more successful ideas are contained in this chapter. Understanding the needs of your pupils and ensuring that they enjoy their lessons with you makes teaching a much more fulfilling experience. Pupils are more likely to be ready to learn so you can get on with what you love: teaching! This links directly back to teacher wellbeing, as a happy class equals a happy teacher. I hope you find something that you can use with your pupils.

Idea 53: Staff versus pupils

Building relationships with pupils and staff alike encourages community spirit.

A good way to focus on wellbeing and to nurture great relationships between staff and pupils is to create a series of competitions across the year that everyone can get involved in. There's no need for them all to be sporty; in fact, if you use the #teacher5aday model you could split the different events across the half terms. The model below is an example of how it might look.

Term 1 – #volunteer
In the first term, time spent volunteering is clocked up, and pupils and staff compete directly with each other. At the end of the term, the winners are announced and prizes won. Examples of volunteering could be taking someone's lesson or helping another pupil with their work, for example. The more hours clocked, the better; hours spent outside of school volunteering should count too. It's amazing how much you find out about pupils when you talk to them about their life outside of school.

Term 2 – #learn
During this term, take part in the Great (insert school name) Knowledge Quiz. This could be tailored to a particular subject or theme for the term. Last year, I created the Great (my school) Literature Quiz. The whole school took part during tutor time; it was a real talking point for the week as tutor groups tried to figure out the answers. Other ideas could include short 100-word story competitions, poetry or even song competitions.

Term 3 – #exercise
The sporty one. Staff versus Pupils (insert sporting activity here). A great way to boost mid-year lethargy! There are often sporting events already taking place at many schools, so why not use them to create a staff versus pupils competition? Sixth formers are particularly keen to be involved, so if you want some organisers, try looking there.

Term 4 – #connect

This idea could be anything from an internet or app competition, to a cross-curricular event like a languages day, for example, where each subject contributes to the theme. The term #connect refers to making connections, whether that be using technology or simply joining people together.

Term 5 – #notice

Create a #notice term where staff and pupils catch people doing good deeds for others. Pupils add names of those caught being helpful to a well-located 'notice' box and staff do the same. The winning side will be the team with the most names in the box. To make this really worthwhile, deliver an assembly at the end, sharing all the good deeds.

Term 6 – celebrate

After all of those competitions, a good idea would be to celebrate the winners. Deliver a final assembly to share all the successes that have happened over the year.

> **Next steps**
> Set up a school team that includes staff and pupils and compete against other schools in your area. Get the local press involved too to share your community spirit.

#teachervpupil
#exercise
#learn
#connect
#notice

Idea 54: Praise, praise, praise

Praise raises pupils' self-esteem and confidence.

It's well known by teachers that pupils respond to praise, but that can be all too easy to forget when you're trying to make your way through a busy week. Often, the effort some pupils go to deserves some special recognition, and what better way to do it than to praise them in some way for their hard work? There are many benefits to praising pupils, aside from them feeling motivated to make better progress. Their confidence builds as we reward their effort, which in turn improves their wellbeing. When we make contact with parents to praise pupils, this has the added benefit of improving communication between the school and home, which helps raise attainment. Below are just some of the ways in which you can recognise pupil effort and success:

- **Notes or phone calls home**: These work really well, as the pupils will receive double praise from both their teacher and their parents or carers.
- **House points, positive points or credits**: Whatever you call them, award them generously and evenly for effort. In one school I worked at we had a weekly target of awards to give out, and I would receive an email informing me of whether I had hit my target. The email also included a breakdown of which classes I had given the awards to. This helped me realise I wasn't always awarding the points evenly.
- **Exercise book recognition**: If you want pupils to have high standards in their exercise books, reward them for doing so. You could share a slide each week that credits anyone whose exercise book is of a high standard with work completed.
- **Assembly awards**: Why not nominate and recognise pupils' effort in whole-school assemblies? The more you create an environment that recognises effort as success, the more pupils will begin to believe they can achieve. This can only mean good things for their wellbeing.

Next steps
As a school, you could consider offering reward trips for those who consistently work hard and put in their best effort. This obviously shouldn't be the only opportunity for pupils to go on a trip, but it will encourage them to work hard, as they will all want to go!

#praisetheeffort
#notice

Idea 55: It starts at the door

A small, simple gesture will ensure pupils know you care.

One of the best purchases I ever made was a self-adhesive whiteboard. I wanted one to stick on my classroom door, initially, with the idea that I could use it to leave messages for any snails who were late to the lesson only to find we had eloped to the computer room (not a common occurrence, thankfully). However, over the years it has become far more useful in a number of ways.

I use it to pose open-ended questions for pupils to ponder as they line up. It works perfectly, as it gives pupils something to do whilst they wait quietly to enter and allows pupils time to seriously consider the question at a deeper level. In short, it promotes higher-order thinking skills. By the time they are settled in the classroom, all the pupils have had time to think and are ready for a full-blown discussion, often about challenging issues or divergent thinking. It also provides the perfect lead to your lesson. Not only that, it makes for a very quick start too.

I also use it to write positive messages to pupils as they arrive. They might have done particularly well in a recent assessment, or they may have exams coming up. The board message cheers them up during times that could be stressful. It's lovely to see their smiles as they read it. Pupils feel a real sense of pride if they receive a special mention too.

The board is used for literacy riddles too. I write the riddle on the board in the morning and pupils from across the school find me during the day to tell me they have figured it out. My younger pupils absolutely love this. They rush to class to be first to see the riddle. Often, I will hand out house points for those who are first to solve it.

You should all have one of these outside your classroom. They promote learning, encourage participation and make pupils feel good. Just watch out for colleagues who think it's funny to draw funky pictures of you on it.

#atthedoor
#learn
#connect

Idea 56: The great outdoors

Taking pupils to outdoor learning spaces brightens their day.

I have been lucky enough to work in schools that have outdoor space in abundance. If there is a way I can get my lessons outside that's creative, enhances learning and promotes wellbeing, I'm in.

The following are just some ideas for how you could use the great outdoors in your lessons.

Mini-assessments and quizzing
Some schools have painted number squares outside that can be used for many activities. If you're doing a mini quiz, go out to the number squares to make it more visual. If pupils get a question correct, they move forward a square. The competitiveness takes hold when pupils see that they're winning. Obviously, the number squares can be used in many ways. Why not think of a use for them in your school?

Reading
One school I worked at had an amphitheatre that was perfect on a summer's day for reading together. In the past, I've even taken pupils out in the fresher months, clad in coats, and told them to lie down on the ground. Not an archaic punishment, but a way to develop empathy for the homeless. We were reading *Stone Cold* by Robert Swindells at the time. Any outdoor space that's quiet can be great for reading lessons.

Writing
What better place to drum up some creative writing than the outdoors? Try taking a class out just to sit and listen; they record sounds, sights, smells, touch and taste, before returning to the classroom with fresh minds and new writing material. Placing pupils in a different setting to their normal classroom can spark real imagination.

Revision
If pupils need to remember facts, use a memory association game by creating a story that's set in the school grounds. This is an idea I learned about during my NQT year, commonly known as the 'memory palace'. The story has links to facts pupils need to learn, but the plot is wildly

eccentric. Once you've read the story to them, walk around the school grounds, remembering the crazy plot, which then triggers the facts. I still have pupils tell me they remember dates and names from years before because of the game. They love it. It works. Winner.

In the past, I have had access to a huge sports field. A stifling classroom, exams looming and past paper overload equals 'rounders revision'. Try taking your class out every year towards the end of revision lessons, equipped with revision apps, paper quizzes and a bat and ball. Then you play rounders and revise at the same time. It can work in many ways; one way in which I have done it is to ask players a question every time they bat. Anyone on a post must quiz any batters that are running around. If they get the question wrong, they remain 'stuck' at that post. The winning team is the team with the most complete runs around the field.

#greatoutdoors
#notice
#exercise

Next steps

If you can't get out, why not bring the outdoors in? In the past, I have done just that. I created a miniature island in the centre of my room out of things I'd collected from outside. Leaves, sand, pebbles and a few shells from the art department made up the island. It was intended as a replica of the island in Lord of the Flies. Pupils were tasked with making a spider's web of revision. Main threads representing characters, theme and plot were connected to the island itself. Pupils made connections with other threads to create a huge web of ideas. They wrote their ideas down on sticky notes and placed them on the string where they thought they best fit. At points throughout the lesson, they were required to justify their thinking. What we were left with at the end of the lesson was quite remarkable. An explosion of ideas all interleaved and connected.

Idea 57: Class mascot

Having a class mascot can really promote positivity amongst pupils.

Allow me to tell you a story that I feel perfectly presents this idea and its benefits. Around seven years ago, I came across a little stuffed toy in a garden centre. He caught my eye because of his insanely huge grin. He came with this message: 'May his joyful smile remind you of all there is to be happy about'. I couldn't resist him.

That little pig is now the infamous Pig of Happiness that has resided in my classroom since that day.

He has provided support to pupils in more ways than I ever thought he would. Firstly, he actually comes with a video on YouTube all about how to spread happiness, which I regularly show the pupils. It's old-fashioned, but they like it.

Secondly, if anyone is feeling a little down or deflated, he becomes their mascot for the lesson. He sits on their desk with his ridiculous grin and they return his smile. In my experience, this works with any age group, even sixth formers! He's an instant mood lifter.

Thirdly, he's often a stimulant for their work. Narratives have involved him. Crime scenes have revolved around him. He even has friends now in the form of other stuffed animals.

It needs to be mentioned that it hasn't always been easy for him. Some pupils (and teachers) have found it funny to kidnap him and send me horrifying images!

It gets much worse, though, and what happened next was all my fault. In the summer of 2014, I travelled across America from the East to the West Coast. I decided to take him with me. The plan was to take photos of him at various landmarks and create a 'Happiness Travels' display when I returned. The pupils were so excited.

It all went terribly wrong on the flight to New York. I was sat with a family travelling back to their home in Pakistan. Three generations of the family greeted me, including a beautiful baby girl of about eight months in age. Approaching JFK, she started to cry. Out of the blue, the grandfather passed her over for me to hold. This worked for a while, but the crying returned. So, I decided to let the pig work his magic. She loved it! The crying stopped and chewing of the pig's ear began. I'll wash him later, I thought.

As we gathered our belongings, I expected them to pass him back. To my horror, he was placed in a bag. The last I saw of him was that familiar smile and a wave as he disappeared down the aisle. A pang of loss ensued. I'd lost the Pig of Happiness. How would I tell the pupils?

In Texas, I bought a cowboy horse to compensate, called him Rusty and took the photos I had planned for the pig. When I told the pupils what had happened, I didn't realise how gutted they'd be. They'd really grown attached to him. I replaced him the following year with a new Pig of Happiness, but it wasn't the same – they call him 'The Imposter'!

This anecdote goes to show how a class mascot can impact the wellbeing of your class. Mascots can be used to improve the mood of your class, as well as provide impetus for learning.

#classmascot
#connect

> ### Next steps
> You could have a mascot for your department, house or whole school and use it to promote healthy competition and positive behaviour. Classes can compete to have the mascot reside in the classroom for the week by winning the most house points or having the best overall attendance, for example.
>
> You could also loan the mascot out to pupils, offering individuals the chance to take it home for a weekend or a half-term break. This instils responsibility in pupils and subtly develops great relationships and trust between teachers and pupils.

Idea 58: Classroom care

Creating a calm learning space promotes pupils' wellbeing and builds their confidence to learn.

A classroom should be an inspiring space. It should be interactive and help to promote learning, as well as being a calm environment that supports pupil wellbeing. It's often best to keep the wall at the front of the classroom free from displays, in order to keep pupils focused on the task at hand when needed, but having classrooms displays elsewhere aids learning, increases enjoyment and encourages pupils to take pride in their work.

One important aim when teaching is to create independent learners. Part of that involves providing learning aids around the room and directing students to make good use of them. Instead of having them ask to leave their desks, try allowing students to get up and help themselves to resources or look for ideas on the displays you have on your walls.

Here are some ideas to help you prepare your classroom so it is a space that inspires and supports learning and pupil wellbeing.

Keywords and vocabulary banks
These will be most useful in subjects where pupils need to remember complex vocabulary and definitions. If we want pupils to use the terminology of our subject areas, we need to expose them to it. Display space is an effective way to do this.

Sentence support
Try including useful sentence starters on your displays to encourage less able pupils to become confident when writing. They can use them to formulate verbal responses and extended writing pieces, particularly analytical essays.

Reflection
You could dedicate some display space to showing the different ways in which pupils can use their green pens for reflection. Using a different coloured pen for student reflection and improvement is a common strategy in many secondary schools. This will enable them to see and understand the value of reflection.

Posters

I love these, and so do the pupils. My posters are based around the subjects I teach (English and law), but you can tailor them to your own subject or school phase. They breathe imagination into the room and serve as useful reminders of past learning.

Pupil work

There's always room for this and you could occupy corridor space too, as pupil work will then get a much wider audience. Instead of throwing away old revision creations, you could frame them, along with a photo of the pupils who made them. This gives pupils a sense of achievement and pride, whilst encouraging others to work hard too.

Another option is to create a 'Wall of Humanity'. This is a working wall containing pupils' thoughts and feelings about particular events that take place throughout the year, such as Remembrance Sunday. Pupils have the opportunity to share their opinions and reflect, and you can add to this whenever you are discussing or reflecting on recent events.

Personalised spaces

Try creating personalised bunting to decorate a specific department or area of the school. In the past, I have decorated the English department with bunting, where each flag featured the front cover of a pupil's favourite book. It's a really effective way of getting pupils talking about a specific subject or skill, such as reading.

Different zones for pupils to use

In your classroom, try creating different zones that pupils can use for information. One example could be a 'stuck station'. If ever a pupil is stuck with their work, they can go and get help in the way of resources from the stuck station. Leave differentiated worksheets, dictionaries and thesauruses there. This will really help to develop pupils' independence.

You could also use spaces as a positive behaviour management tool. Something your students will love is a 'comfy corner'. This can consist of two comfy chairs (taken stealthily from the staffroom) and two bookcases filled with books. Pupils can then take it in turns to sit there and read during reading lessons. You can use it as a reward for exemplary effort too and it will become a place that pupils will work hard to get to.

#classroomcare
#notice

Idea 59: Beyond the classroom

Extra-curricular activities develop positive relationships with pupils and promote wellbeing.

One of the best ways to build positive relationships with your pupils is to get to know them beyond the confined space of your classroom. Over the years, I have taken part in many extra-curricular activities. I have found time and time again that the relationships I have with the pupils I teach have been made stronger by doing so. Getting to know pupils in this way encourages them to be confident learners too, as they naturally become more comfortable with you. Here are some of the ways in which you can get involved.

School trips

Trips are a great way to get pupils involved in your subject or a topic you are teaching. I have taken pupils to the Houses of Parliament and the Old Bailey as part of their law course, and visited the Somme Battlefields and read war poetry from the exact spot it was written during World War One. I have also taken part in Year 7 adventure trips to the Ardèche region in France and visited the theatre many times with my English literature pupils. What better way to promote your subject and ensure pupils are enjoying themselves? Why not think about a trip that you could help out on?

Clubs

Why not set up a club for pupils in your school? Of course, if you wish, it can be relevant to your teaching – for example a reading club – but it doesn't have to be. I know teachers who have set up choirs, baking clubs and gaming clubs. The benefits are clear; pupils are engaging in activities beyond the classroom and this creates a healthy balance of work and play. Why not set up a club or attend a current club to develop your relationship with your pupils?

Competitions

Whether they be whole-school competitions or just small competitions within your area, these are great for engaging pupils and encouraging participation. Pupils develop a sense of pride in their work, which makes them feel good about themselves. In the past, I have run literacy competitions, house competitions and even competitions to raise money for charities. What could you create in your school to promote pupil wellbeing?

Charity work

Bringing pupils together to raise money for charity encourages good values in pupils and it also helps to develop good relationships between teachers and pupils. As a form tutor and eventually a head of house, I regularly encouraged my form to get involved in charity work. Seeing them take responsibility for raising funds and orchestrate fundraising events was wonderful to watch. Often, I would make phone calls to parents to praise a pupil's efforts, which, in turn, contributed to excellent relationships. Why not see if there are any local charities that need support and consider whether you and your pupils can contribute by fundraising in some way? It is joint enterprises like these that help to forge effective relationships and develop communities within schools.

Next steps

Before you set up your own trip, club or competition, it is a good idea to find out what your school already offers. Is there a space for what you would like to set up? It might also be worth attending an extra-curricular event at your school to see how things work before you decide what type of activity you would like to promote.

#extrateacher
#volunteer
#learn

Idea 60: The cupboard of curiosity

Props promote curiosity and encourage pupils to take part.

I absolutely love props. If I think they can interest the pupils and add value to the lesson, I use them. Part of taking care of the wellbeing of pupils is ensuring that they enjoy lessons and learning. The list below suggests just a few items you could use to promote curiosity and encourage enjoyment in your classroom.

- **Masks and wigs**: Pupils can use these when taking part in role plays or performing scenes from plays. You could offer them as a reward if they volunteer to read bigger parts.
- **Sticky notes**: These are cheap, colourful and easy to use, whether it be for assessment planning or creating connections between ideas. Another reason why they are so great is they are quick to use and can be stuck anywhere, from your whiteboard to your windows. The fact that they come in different colours also helps when pupils are organising their ideas.
- **Balloons**: In the past, I've made hot air balloons, suspended them from the ceiling, told the pupils that we needed to escape danger and that only ten of them could go. In role, they use their persuasive devices to get on the balloon. I took this idea from Rhea Fallows, Head of English at a previous school I worked at. I've also included them in giant revision webs that we've made.
- **Timers and bells**: A whole variety of timers live in my classroom – sand ones, liquid ones and even giant bombs. They are useful for quizzes and tasks that need to be timed for pace. I also have three service bells that we use in a similar way.
- **String**: This is always useful. One way you can use it is to make giant spider's webs to develop subject knowledge and connect ideas together. It's brilliant to watch the pupils learn in such a collaborative way. Be warned though, if you don't control this activity with specific instructions, it can get a little messy.
- **Play dough**: This is useful for revision activities. Pupils make something from whatever it is they are revising and other pupils have to

guess what it is. One of my law pupils made an entire revision video using it!

- **Hats**: Pupils love hats. They're obsessed. They come in during lunch just to wear them. In lessons, try placing them on pupils' heads when they arrive, knowing that you want to ask particular questions to certain pupils. They know that if they have one on, they'll be called upon in some way. It prepares them to be brave and it subtly differentiates your lesson.
- **Pegs**: These are great for timelines, ordering events, justifying ideas and for hanging up great pupil work. You can also place them on pupils' desks as a way of differentiating, just like in the hats idea.
- **Poster paper**: You can use this for making huge revision mind maps. Pupils work together using only their minds to create these. They're great visuals but will usually need to be displayed in the corridor because they are so big!
- **Handcuffs**: These are a totally innocent prop that I use for court scenes with my law pupils. However, I did have some explaining to do when an anti-terrorism police officer found them in my locker once. They were doing a safety search before we had the Olympic torch pass through the school. Oops!
- **Glass pens**: These are great for adding a bit of variety to your lessons. If you prefer pupils' work to be in books in normal lessons, you could use them for revision activities. You can use them to write on windows, but also on desks, as it washes off easily. Pupils absolutely love them.
- **Mini whiteboards**: You can use these for low-stakes quizzes at the beginning of a lesson to test pupils on previous knowledge. They are great because you get instant feedback about which pupils have picked up ideas from the previous lessons and which are less confident.

This is not an exhaustive list, but even if you try a few of these props out with your class, it will help create a positive environment for pupils and will encourage imagination in your classes.

Next steps

Consider how you can promote curiosity in your lessons. What items would the pupils find interesting? How would they add value to the learning journey of your pupils and encourage enjoyment at the same time? The key is only to include them if they add to the learning. Avoid using props just for the sake of it.

#propsforlearning
#learn
#connect

Idea 61: Creativity chaos

Allowing pupils the chance to be creative encourages enthusiasm for learning.

Every so often in my English lessons, I like to give the pupils a task that allows them to be a little creative. It's a chance for them to demonstrate their understanding, or even to simply engage with the topic in a way they feel comfortable with. The task is usually set for homework and pupils are offered a choice of activities to complete.

Here are some ideas to help you encourage creativity amongst your pupils:

- **Cakes**: Pupils love to bake. In the past, I have received cake models of the Globe Theatre and even World War One trenches. They're great as additional homework tasks.
- **Poems**: Encourage pupils to demonstrate their understanding by writing a poem. Obviously, this works well in English lessons, but it's also a great way to demonstrate any knowledge.
- **Songs**: These work in the same way as poems but have the added bonus of being sung in lessons, which always generates a few smiles.
- **Costumes**: Ask pupils to design or even make costumes for characters in books they are studying.
- **Imagery tasks**: Many pupils like to recreate scenes from books or plays we have studied using their own images. They love the chance to express their ideas in such a visual way. I've had paintings of scenes from *A Midsummer Night's Dream*, drawings of Eva Smith from *An Inspector Calls* and many more great pieces of art.

The one thing you will notice is the sheer amount of pride the pupils display when they bring their completed projects in.

#creativitychaos
#learn
#connect

Next steps
If you aren't ready to give pupils completely free rein, why not control their projects a little? Ask pupils to summarise a topic in 50 words, then ask them to reduce the words to 25, and eventually, after some more reductions, ask them to choose just one word. Every pupil then writes their word on the board. For their creative projects, the pupils must focus on the 30 keywords collated to ensure they are demonstrating the right knowledge.

Idea 62: Music motivation

Music is food for the soul; use it wisely to manage your pupils' wellbeing.

Music is powerful. We all have a soundtrack or type of music we like to listen to depending on our mood. Below are some suggestions of how to use music to improve your mood or ignite some thought-provoking ideas in lessons or assemblies:

- Allow pupils the freedom to create songs about the topic they are studying. Often, I set homework projects that allow for this kind of creative response. Students can show real understanding of a topic in this way and it often leads to some surprising ideas.
- Use music in your lessons to get pupils thinking. For example, you could play songs in your lesson as pupils are entering the room and ask them to make a connection between songs and particular characters in a book. It gets them thinking before the lesson has even fully begun. You could also play music from a particular period in time to suit the topic you are studying. It can help pupils understand the topic in more depth.
- Use music in assemblies to set the tone for the theme you have chosen. As a Head of House, I would spend all year taking photographs of my house pupils' achievements just so I could create a video for them to watch at the end of the year. Choosing the right song really does have an impact on a significant number of pupils. I've seen some cry with joy at what they have achieved and, no doubt, the chosen music has had a role to play.

#musictherapy
#notice
#connect

Idea 63: Revision recovery bags

Showing your pupils you care works wonders.

This idea came from a wonderful history teacher called Lesley Munro (@LesleyMunro4) and I have since adapted it to suit my own classes. The aim of the activity is for pupils to feel valued and prepared in the weeks running up to external exams.

You'll first need to get yourself some brown paper bags. Lesley included a number of items inside them:

- **A5 sheets with suggestions for revision strategies** – I usually tell my pupils to focus on quizzing, mind maps and flash cards, as they have repeatedly been shown to be the most successful activities for revision.
- **A bookmark** – one for each topic or exam paper, which gives the breakdown of what is required for each question, timings and how many marks are available.
- **Another bookmark** – this time with QR codes that take pupils straight to the revision guides on the school's website and to other useful revision resources.
- **Sticky tabs** – these are used to mark pages in revision books.
- **A pen** – for obvious reasons.
- **A highlighter** – as above!
- **A little bag of sweets** – to keep pupils going during the long revision days.
- **A loyalty card** – pupils receive a sticker for their card for every revision session or intervention session they attend, for outstanding class work or for outstanding behaviour. They can redeem the card for prizes.

I added the following items to my own bags:

- **Knowledge organisers** – these are A4-sized and contain everything pupils need to know about a particular topic. Many teachers make these themselves, but a quick search on Google and you will find lots of pre-made examples. They're brilliant revision resources. You can find out more about them by reading this blog by Joe Kirby, Deputy Headteacher at Michaela School:

https://pragmaticreform.wordpress.com/2015/03/28/knowledge-organisers

- **Sticky notes** – I added a load of these to each bag so pupils could use them for revision.
- **A small note for each pupil** – you can include words of encouragement for them to reflect on.
- **A party popper** – I allow pupils to use these at the end of our very last lesson. Again, seeing them smile after all of their hard work is great. It requires a bit of tidying up after!

You can add all of the above items to your bags or find a combination that works for you and your pupils. Whatever you include, pupils will feel valued and ready to tackle the exam season.

> **Next steps**
> If you want pupils to really feel valued, why not create a poem about the class? I do this every year. Seeing their faces light up when they get their own special mention in the poem is just wonderful, and as an added bonus, you have a little reminder yourself of each class you have taught.

#revisionrecovery
#connect
#notice

Idea 64: Keeping it calm

Controlling the noise level in your classroom supports pupil wellbeing and learning.

As teachers, it is our responsibility to ensure pupils feel comfortable enough to learn in our classrooms. One of the most important things you can do for pupils in your lessons is to keep the learning environment calm and controlled. Some pupils can find it incredibly stressful if the noise level in your classroom is too high. It can hamper their learning as well as distress them.

A great way to monitor noise during group work is by using the Bouncy Balls app (bouncyballs.org). This app was shared by Martin Burrett (@ICTMagic) at a TeachMeet I organised. It allows users to monitor the level of noise in a room by showing balls bouncing. The higher they bounce, the louder the noise level in the room. You can change the balls to eyeballs, emojis or bubbles. It's a great visual tool to help pupils understand the importance of moderating their voice.

Often, you may wish for the pupils to be working hard on their own. I insist on silence whenever pupils are doing independent work. If you want pupils to be silent, you must ask them to be *silent*, not quiet. By asking the pupils to be quiet, you are suggesting that they can make some level of noise, which sends the wrong instruction. In every lesson, I have at least 20 minutes of silence. The pupils have no need to be talking, as the work they have completed prior to this has led to them being able to work on their own. You will find that pupils are able to concentrate far better in this kind of learning environment and feel much calmer. They also get much more work done and, therefore, they make quicker progress. Don't be afraid to insist on silence.

#keepcalmteacher
#learn

Idea 65: Pupil leadership

Allocating pupils leadership roles encourages responsibility and independence.

Pupils develop as young people when we give them responsibility. As a teacher, not only does this build trust between yourself and your pupils, but it also has the benefit of making your life a little easier too! There are many ways in which schools can do this at a whole-school level, but as a class teacher, you can encourage pupil leadership too.

- Assign roles to each pupil. Stephen Lockyer has this idea nailed with his wonderful invention, the class job wheel. On the wheel is a list of jobs, together with the class list, which means that jobs are rotated each week and, over the year, every pupil will have done each job.
- When pupils begin in your class each year, assign them numbers. You can then give them a specific responsibility each lesson. At the beginning and end of the lesson, for example, you could ask the '2s' to distribute or collect in the exercise books. This is rotated across all groups evenly. (Pupils can also stay in these numbers for group work, which eliminates any arguing and allows for a quick start to tasks).
- As a form tutor, roles can also be distributed across your tutees. Have someone responsible for collecting the reading books. Allow some to take care of classroom displays, shelves or plants. Rotate these roles throughout the year using the job wheel.
- Nominate class reading leaders. Pair up stronger readers with less confident readers. This has the added benefit of developing relationships between pupils too.
- Choose some pupils to be homework leaders. Allow them the opportunity to help others with homework when they are stuck or struggling. Again, this supports relationships and independence.
- Appoint table or group leaders and encourage them to take a leading role in activities. They will experience leadership of their peers, which will develop their confidence and communication skills.

#leaders
#volunteer
#connect

> **Next steps**
> Perhaps you would like to get involved in pupil leadership at a whole-school level. Why not volunteer to run a pupil leadership programme? You can link it to the pastoral curriculum in your school.

Chapter 6

Community care

Schools are part of a much bigger picture. Build links with your local community and watch your pupils flourish.

If you think the community outside the school gates has no impact on pupil and staff wellbeing inside the school, think again. By developing positive relationships with every stakeholder, you are building a community that cares about the place where you work. The links forged by this process offer schools great reputations amongst locals, which, in turn, makes your teaching life much easier. A sense of pride is shared by all, including the pupils, who feel happy in their much-loved school. This sense of pride impacts on individual teacher wellbeing, as you know that the school you are proud to work in is celebrated by others too. It can be a very different story if the opposite occurs. Working in a school with a less than desirable reputation can be challenging and can often leave your wellbeing in tatters. One school I worked at really understood this point. They went to great lengths to encourage the local community to feel welcome in the school. As teachers, we were asked to develop frequent communication with parents too, making our lives much easier come parents' evening. This chapter contains ideas about how to enhance wellbeing in schools by growing stronger connections with the local community. There are ideas about how to reach out to local businesses, as well as looking for places to display pupil work outside of the school walls. Ideas about how to get the local community into your schools are also included here. I would love to hear all about how you are making stronger community links if you would like to share your stories with me on Twitter. Use the hashtags at the end of each idea to get in touch.

Idea 66: Love your library

Building links with your local library develops wellbeing for staff and pupils.

Local libraries are fantastic resources. However, with budget cuts over recent years, there have been closures and a decline in availability across the country. As schools, we can support our local libraries in a number of ways and build strong community links whilst doing so. Libraries are a hive of activity and whilst many of us are happy to visit purely for the books, some of our pupils may need a little encouragement to attend for other reasons. Here are some ways you can use the library to your advantage.

Librarian visits
Why not ask your local librarian to visit the school and deliver an assembly on what the library has to offer? This may encourage the more reluctant pupils to become more involved with reading and studying.

Class visits
It's vital that we express the importance of books and reading to our pupils. Librarians can support us with this aim. Why not arrange a class visit and show your pupils just how much the library has to offer?

Exhibitions
Libraries are a fantastic way to show off your pupils' talents. They regularly hold exhibitions and they might be willing to display pupils' work. Encourage parents to visit and it's a great opportunity to showcase the school and network simultaneously. Contact your local library to see what they have on offer.

Extra-curricular events
Libraries hold many extra-curricular events. Poetry evenings, music nights and creative writing courses are usually available and there's often much more on offer too. Why not attend yourself and build those community links? Better still, encourage your pupils to go along too.

Next steps
Connect your school librarian with the local librarian to develop better links and arrange bespoke events for your pupils. The more connections you make, the easier it will be to encourage your pupils to read and develop their learning.

#librarylover
#connect
#learn
#volunteer

Idea 67: Events nights

Inviting the wider community into the school environment will develop strong relationships with all stakeholders.

One way to involve the local community in school life is to hold events nights. These can be as imaginative as you like. Here are some ideas for you to think about.

Quiz nights
These are obviously great fun. Invite parents and local businesses along, as well as staff from the school. In my experience the more teams that attend the better. Be warned, it can get very competitive.

Music nights
There will undoubtedly be some budding stars amongst the pupils in your school, but what about their parents? Why not have music nights where the local community is invited along to take part and show off their musical ability? These can be competition-based or even held over a weekend like a mini festival.

Talent shows
These aren't just fun for the pupils. Why not get the parents involved too? They are hilariously funny!

Awards ceremonies
These are usually held at the end of a school year. Invite parents and local businesses along to award ceremonies for your pupils. It's wonderful for them to see what young people have achieved over the year and, more importantly, what they have to offer the local community.

Next steps
Why not ask local businesses to sponsor your events nights and donate prizes for them? This will develop even stronger local links and promote both the school and the local economy.

#eventsplanner
#connect
#volunteer

Idea 68: Careers talks

Bringing together the learning world and the working world gives pupils direction.

When I was at school, I remember having a meeting with a careers advisor about what I wanted to do for a living. I told her I wanted to be a primary teacher, at which point she gave me plenty of advice about other careers involving working with children. That was the only piece of information I ever received about moving on from education. As kind as the lady was, it felt a little vague and left me with more questions than answers. Luckily, since working in schools, I've seen much more proactive attempts at helping pupils choose a career path.

A great way to avoid a lack of information for pupils is to hold careers talks at school. Professionals from all fields can come in and deliver assemblies or workshops to those who have an interest in that particular field.

There are many benefits to this idea. Firstly, it provides pupils with first-hand information from experts in their fields. They get to hear about the ins and outs of working life from someone who actually experiences it on a daily basis. What better way to learn about a job or profession you are interested in? Secondly, it allows parents to become involved too. Invite them in to give their take on the jobs they have. You will be surprised how many of them volunteer to take part. Thirdly, local businesses will also be grateful for an invite. They get to share their own local knowledge and expertise, as well as promote their own businesses to potential employees.

What a brilliant idea to forge great relationships between the school and its surrounding community!

Next steps

Why not develop a work experience programme with the businesses in the local area? Too many schools are now forsaking this element of education in favour of more curriculum time in lessons. This experience can be hugely influential to pupils and help them make decisions about their chosen career paths. See Idea 74 for more on this.

#careertalks
#connect
#learn
#volunteer

Idea 69: Elderly love

Forging links with the elderly in the local community develops empathy amongst pupils and builds strong relationships for all.

This idea really does come from the heart. As a child in primary school, I remember going along to a local residential home at Christmas and meeting the residents. We would sing Christmas carols for them and play games. It was one of the best times of the year and to see so many elderly people with smiles on their faces was wonderful. As a teacher, I believe schools have a responsibility to make links with the local elderly community. Here are some ideas to get you thinking:

- **Christmas lunch**: Try inviting local elderly residents to a free Christmas lunch. The pupils can help cook the meals in their food technology lessons and then serve it too. You could also have performers from school to entertain the guests. It is such a great way to immerse two generations of people who may never really meet in such a way otherwise.
- **Christmas visits**: As already mentioned, taking a group of pupils to visit a residential home and sing some carols for the elderly residents is such a heart-warming activity. Both pupils and residents genuinely feel good for taking part.
- **Dance evenings**: These can take place at any time of the year and give elderly residents the opportunity to socialise and get some exercise whilst they take part.
- **Special invites to school concerts or productions**: School productions and concerts take place every year in most schools. There is usually a matinee for other local schools to come along and watch. Why not put on an extra show at the end of your production for local elderly residents?

Next steps
Consider creating more lasting links by contacting your local elderly residents' homes to see if they would like to take part in a pen friend system. Pupils write letters to their chosen pen pal during tutor time and the elderly residents write back. Imagine the joy created when they each receive their letters!

#elderlylove
#volunteer
#connect
#exercise

Idea 70: Facility-friendly school

Allowing everyone access to school resources promotes excellent community links.

Schools are quite privileged in that they often have access to some amazing resources. In some of the schools I've worked in, I've been lucky enough to have access to state-of-the-art sports halls, all kinds of sporting equipment, modern IT suites, excellent learning resource centres, dance studios, drama studios, large open spaces (both indoors and out), gyms and fitness suites, and endless grassy fields. In my opinion, it would be a shame if these amazing resources weren't shared with the local community. In most schools that I've worked in, the spaces have been available for the local community to hire. This has the added benefit of building those all-important links with parents and supporting businesses. Here are some of the ways in which the spaces could be used:

- **Dance lessons**: The dance studio could be hired out by a local dance teacher for private lessons.
- **IT courses**: IT courses for adult learners could make good use of an IT suite.
- **Sporting activities**: These can of course be varied but badminton evenings, Zumba classes, tennis lessons and use of the fitness suite have all been available at schools where I have worked.
- **Use of the playing field**: The field could be made available to hire for other local schools and town-wide sporting events.
- **Music lessons**: Peripatetic music teachers could use schools as bases for their lessons.

Obviously, it is down to individual people as to what could take place at your school, but by making the facilities available, you are extending the arm of friendship between the school and its surrounding community. So, what are you waiting for?

#facilityfriendly
#connect
#learn

Idea 71: Charity champions

Raising money for charity encourages community spirit amongst pupils.

This idea is pretty much a given in all schools. All of the schools I've worked in have, at some point, raised money for charity, whether it be a small cake sale or a much grander event such as a charity concert. I was lucky enough to work in one school where charity fundraising was at the heart of the pastoral house system. As a head of house, I was given the opportunity to choose a charity to be affiliated with my house. I chose a local children's hospice. I'll never forget the feeling of being able to raise a significant amount of money for such a worthy cause.

If your school isn't already raising money for charity, consider some of the ideas below:

- **Formalise the fundraising**: Attach charities to the pastoral curriculum through the house or college system in your school. Make a competition out of it to see which tutor groups and houses make the most for their chosen charity.
- **Cake sales**: Why not allow pupils the opportunity to raise money for charity in this way? Macmillan Coffee Morning is a good place to start.
- **Sponsored events**: These can be held on celebration days or at the end of the year to raise money for local charities.
- **Awareness days**: Charities like Comic Relief, Children in Need and Save the Children all rely heavily on schools taking part in their events, and pupils love the red noses, spotty clothing and Christmas jumper days too.
- **Support local charities**: Find out what local charities there are in your area and see if you can raise funds for them. They rely on their local community to support their cause much more than the larger charities and are working on shoestring budgets doing incredible things.

#charitymatters
#volunteer
#connect

Idea 72: Volunteer projects

Volunteering is an essential part of a supportive community.

One of the key principles behind the #teacher5aday work is volunteering. As teachers, we volunteer to help out our colleagues all the time. Outside of work, there are plenty of opportunities to volunteer help in many organisations. Encouraging volunteering amongst our pupils is a great way to show them how to be an active member of the community, whilst also strengthening relationships between the local area and the school community. Why not set up a volunteering scheme at your school? This could be embedded into the pastoral curriculum, and classes, houses, tutor groups or colleges could earn points and prizes for the number of hours they volunteer to help others. This could be hours volunteered for activities in school or activities they have taken part in outside of school. Here are some ideas you could try:

In school

- **Litter picking**: Classes or tutor groups take part in litter picking on rotation and points can be awarded to those who collect the most rubbish.
- **Lunch service support**: Allow pupils to help out in the canteen when lunch is being served.
- **Library assistants**: Some pupils absolutely love to spend time in the library.
- **Reception assistant**: Give pupils the opportunity to work on the reception desk. Some pupils love taking part and having a sense of responsibility.
- **Animal care**: Why not ask pupils to volunteer to care for school pets or animals?
- **Sports assistants**: Some pupils love to volunteer their time in the PE department.

Outside of school

- **Supermarket bag packing**: Contact your local supermarkets to see if you and your pupils can volunteer to bag pack for the day.

Supermarkets are always willing to help, especially if you are also raising money for charity.

- **Marshalling events**: There are plenty of opportunities to volunteer at local events by marshalling and directing visitors.
- **Museums**: Some museums are run solely by volunteers. Contact your local museum to see if they need a hand.
- **Libraries**: Likewise, many libraries are now run by volunteers. Perhaps they could do with some support too.
- **Volunteer organisations**: Head to www.gov.uk/government/get-involved/take-part/volunteer for many more volunteering opportunities both locally and nationally.

Next steps

Why not nominate individuals or your own school for the British Volunteer Awards and have your pupils' hard work recognised?

#volunteer
#connect
#learn

Idea 73: Open school policy

Having an open school provides a sense of community and improves communication.

Often, schools go to great lengths to let the community know that they operate under an open school policy. Yet I wonder how many of them truly do? One element of an open school is an open door policy. These have been around for years. The idea is that all doors to all offices remain open throughout the day, particularly those of school leaders, so that staff can communicate with them if they want to. My current headteacher does this every day and there is certainly a more informal feel to our school environment. Other benefits include:

- It encourages effective communication between leadership and staff.
- Staff are less likely to feel left out and more likely to feel supported.
- When people directly communicate with each other, there is no room for the confusion that can often occur in schools.
- It promotes healthy discussion and allows staff the opportunity to speak freely to their line managers if an issue arises.

Another element to open schools is an open door policy for teachers. Encouraging teachers to leave their classroom doors open during lessons can result in a more supportive environment and greater trust between teachers and leadership. If staff are reluctant to try this, perhaps an open door week could be introduced at first. You may also wonder why staff are reluctant, in which case ask yourself if there is something more the school can do to support teachers. A school with a blame culture may well see problems like this.

Finally, if a school is truly open, it invites the community into its buildings at every opportunity. Can parents come and visit the school in action or are they only allowed to visit during an open evening? Many parents prefer to see lessons taking place and get the general feel of a school during a normal school day. Open schools that provide this opportunity build stronger links with the community and it also shows they are proud of their school and what it has to offer.

#openschools
#connect

Idea 74: Work experience survival

Work experience for pupils supports local businesses whilst developing pupils' skills.

In England, the current law states that young people must stay in education until they are 18. This changed from age 16 in 2008. Since then, more and more schools have decided to take away the opportunity for pupils to undergo work experience in the local community. This, of course, was also brought about, in part, by the recent GCSE overhaul, which placed time constraints on teachers in terms of delivering the content required for the new exams. As a result of this, bonds that were perhaps strong between local businesses and schools have weakened and pupils are not being offered the chance to develop their skills in a profession of interest.

This is a disappointing trend, as pupils found work experience to be valuable. Many would decide on their chosen career path on the basis of these experiences. As a 16-year-old, I myself went to a primary school to do work experience. I still remember it to this day. The act of being treated like an adult, coupled with the sense of responsibility I felt, was a powerful determiner of my future and, after a few about turns, here I am as a teacher.

If schools are serious about supporting their pupils and developing them as adults, they should continue to run work experience weeks for them. What other opportunity provides them with such a fully immersive experience? When else will pupils get the opportunity to experience a job before they are actually doing it? Never, in most cases. Not only that, it helps to develop strong links with local community businesses. These businesses may, in turn, support the school when they need it, for example at charity events.

#workexperiencesurvival
#connect
#learn

Idea 75: Supporting support staff

Support staff are the backbone of all schools. Let's make sure we support them too.

I had quite a long, but not uncommon, route into teaching. I began as a youth worker, before getting my first job in a school as a teaching assistant (TA). Following that, I became a behaviour manager and then an unqualified teacher. I was finally accepted onto the Graduate Teacher Programme after completing an English literature course in my spare time. It's fair to say that I experienced a variety of support roles.

Throughout my time as a member of support staff, I learned many things, not least that support staff play a vital role in schools. Without them, where would we be? Who would support your pupils when they need it most? Who would help you prepare resources even when they really don't have to? Who would cook the meals in school? Who would let you pay for lunch tomorrow because you left your money at home again? Who would make sure your classrooms are safe to teach in? Who would fix your radiators so you aren't frozen in your office? Who would empty your bins each day and clean your tables and floor? Who would make sure you are paid on time?

Yet with all of this information known to everyone, why is it that support staff often go unnoticed in schools? Or are seen as secondary to teachers? As schools, we should be celebrating every part of our community, support staff included. Here are some ways that this can be done:

- **Training**: Despite support staff valuing their work, they can often feel undertrained for their role. Schools have a responsibility to train all staff members so that they feel confident to do their role well.
- **In-house training**: Instead of saying, 'Support staff are not needed this evening' or 'Support staff need not attend', invite them along if they wish. How about saying something like 'Whilst support staff are under no obligation to attend this afternoon's training, all are welcome'? A person can feel very excluded if a message is taken out of context. A little care and thought may be required. As a head of

house, I remember two TAs (who were attached to my house) once thanking me for inviting them along to every briefing, as TAs in other houses had been told not to attend. A well-meaning teacher may have tried to save them some time in doing so, but the invite should have been made nonetheless.

- **Emails**: Include support staff in emails that they may find useful. If they are attached to your department, have their name added to the group email. These small changes can mean the world of difference to a TA who supports in your lessons.
- **Schemes of learning**: Share schemes of learning and resources in advance so TAs know what they are doing before the lesson itself. If this isn't done, it can really hamper the progress of pupils and leave the TA feeling frustrated that they couldn't do more to help.
- **Social gatherings**: Invite support staff to social events. This really helps to bring the school community together.
- **Equal treatment**: Treat TAs as your equal in front of the pupils. If pupils understand that the teacher and the TA have equal status, they are less likely to misbehave for the TA. This will also empower the TA in their role. They may then feel comfortable following the behaviour policy without asking you to support them. This may seem obvious but I've seen examples of where this hasn't been done and it's not nice for anyone involved.
- **Say thank you**: Openly thank support staff in front of pupils. This demonstrates their importance in the school and will encourage pupils to do the same. Without adults modelling the behaviour we want to see in pupils, nothing will change.
- **Give praise**: Openly praise support staff to their line managers. If they are doing a great job, let them know about it. If you don't, who will? Support staff are notoriously humble about the work they do.
- **Wellbeing awards**: Include support staff in wellbeing awards. This seems obvious but if staff don't realise they can nominate support staff, why would they?
- **School trips**: Invite support staff on school trips. As we all know, support staff pay isn't great. Why not add some perks to their job by inviting them on a school trip?

#supportstars
#notice
#connect

Idea 76: Create a community resource map

Knowing what resources exist in the local area will support stronger community links.

How do we expect to make better connections with the local community if we don't know what's available? Some schools are geographically close to huge corporations and businesses, yet have very little contact with them or, worse, don't even know they exist. One idea to combat this is for schools to create a community resource map that contains everything you need to know about the local area: businesses, outdoor learning opportunities, local primary schools, local secondary school, nurseries, school trip possibilities and so on. Having this bespoke local directory is hugely beneficial when you are seeking support or would like to develop stronger community links.

As part of the process of building your map, you should contact local businesses to see what resources and support they can offer for free or at a discount. Likewise, you should also find out if they offer work experience opportunities to pupils. Contact local independent charities too. They may wish to support school fundraising events and, in turn, the school may wish to raise funds for a charity in their local area. Some companies may wish to be involved in the curriculum by offering experiences linked to specific subject areas. They may even decide to come in and deliver career talks. All too often, pupils ask in lessons, 'When am I ever going to need this?' Making curriculum links with local businesses can help them to make connections between what they are learning in school and the world of work. Making links with local schools can prove to be a positive act. It counteracts the competitive element that has so unwelcomely taken over in recent years by ensuring schools work together for the good of all pupils, not just their own.

Essentially, the more contact you make with different members of the community, the easier it becomes to collaborate in the future. This kind of networking really does promote effective communities.

#communityresourcemap
#connect
#learn

Idea 77: Wellbeing committee

Wellbeing is everyone's responsibility. All should be involved.

Some schools now have a wellbeing committee who meet regularly to discuss how we can look after the wellbeing of our staff. It's wonderful, as ideas come from the teachers themselves and a number of events are delivered across the year as a result. I love that wellbeing remains a focus throughout the year and it's really positive that so many teachers are involved in promoting it.

However, schools are part of a much wider community. If we really are serious about wellbeing, why not have a committee that is open to parents and local businesses too? Developing wellbeing on a larger scale could be so beneficial for the school and surrounding community. I envision the following process:

1. Schools advertise the wellbeing committee on their website, via school communications systems to parents and by contacting local businesses.
2. If people would like to take part, they can express their interest and go through a similar process to that of becoming a governor. This would ensure that everyone involved takes their role seriously.
3. Once the committee is in place, dates can be set for meetings. A committee leader could plan the agenda for each meeting based on the community's current needs. Wouldn't it be brilliant to be able to support local needs as well as the needs of teachers within the school? Here are some of the possibilities:
   - Quiz nights – the local community takes part too.
   - Charity fundraising events – local businesses support as sponsors.
   - School fundraising events – again with local sources as sponsors.
   - Teacher retreats – taking teachers away for a relaxing weekend.
   - Sports competitions – teachers versus parents would make for excellent entertainment!

These are just a few ideas, but the possibilities are endless and will, of course, be based on the context of individual schools and their locations.

#communitywellbeing
#connect

Chapter 7

Whole–school wellbeing

School leaders have a responsibility to ensure that the wellbeing of their staff and pupils is supported.

I don't think there's anyone working in schools who won't agree that this is an important topic. All too often, I've heard about people's experiences of working in schools where headteachers and the senior leadership team are hell-bent on progress, pushing forward with new initiatives with little concern about the impact it all has on their staff and pupils. Unfortunately, I have experienced this first-hand too. Statistics about teachers leaving the profession and facts and figures about teacher stress levels are worryingly high. School leaders have a responsibility to ensure that their teams are well looked after. After all, an unhappy, burnt-out teacher is no good to anybody, least of all pupils. This chapter is full of ideas about how school leaders can make a difference to the wellbeing of staff and pupils alike. It contains ideas about report writing and how to bring a school together, and ideas about responsible teaching and learning responsibilities (TLRs). If you are a headteacher or school leader, I hope there is something useful in it for you. If you aren't a school leader but see something you like, why not suggest it at your next meeting? Be brave and support the wellbeing of everyone.

Idea 78: Report writing

Managing staff time is essential for their wellbeing, so is report writing absolutely essential?

During my early teaching years, there were certain points throughout the academic year where I spent long hours of an evening writing detailed, individual reports for the many pupils I taught – often in the hundreds. I gave up weekends and dedicated time outside of normal working hours to complete this arduous task. Admittedly, I had a bank of phrases I would use to get through the process and many reports looked similar to those of other pupils in my class. As I reluctantly typed, I often wondered whether there was a better way to present this information to parents. Of course, it's important to inform parents of their children's progress but surely there is a more efficient way? It seems to me that what parents want to know is whether their child is supported and, as a result, is making great progress. This activity remains a pressure point for many teachers today. I know that many schools still insist on writing individual reports for every child in the school, especially in primary settings, but it takes place in secondary schools too.

One school I worked at was different. I was thrilled when they told me that they had done away with report writing. 'Did parents not complain?' I enquired. 'No' was the resounding answer. So how did this new school report to parents and give detailed feedback about each child's progress? The idea was simple. Teachers provided data points throughout the year and a more detailed report on parents' evening. Currently, many schools already report data at three points throughout the year. If this isn't enough for parents to know how well their child is performing, what is? Being free from writing reports also saves teachers hours and hours of time, so that they can actually get on with planning great lessons and developing the progress of their pupils.

Another idea to support this would be to hold regular open hours, face to face or via the telephone, across the year. These informal drop-ins could replace the hours spent writing reports, and parents with concerns could get a quick response to their query.

This makes perfect sense to me. Why spend time writing down information that you are likely to say upon meeting parents face to face? Leaders of schools who are serious about managing the workload of their staff should challenge unnecessary tasks like this at every opportunity. Why not try it for a year and see the visible difference it makes?

#nomorereports
#connect

Next steps

This idea is about report writing but there are other underlying issues here too. Should we be reporting data so frequently given that there has been so much change, particularly in secondary schools, in the way we assess our pupils? My feeling is that with the many changes schools currently face, we should be very cautious about reporting so frequently to parents. There is a danger here of providing too much information that may not be entirely accurate. Pupils' progress is not always linear and often it can take more than a term to see real evidence of progress. Why not review the way you communicate with parents on a much larger scale? See Ideas 79 and 88 about data and parents' evenings for more information.

Idea 79: Data dilemmas

Managing the amount of data staff use is crucial to avoid information overload and to improve time efficiency.

Back when the National Curriculum levels were introduced in the 1980s, there was only ever an expectation that schools reported pupils' achievement at the end of each key stage. This data reflected their progress over time. Now, for many reasons, not least the idea that everything we do in schools must be measured, we seem to have gone completely over the top. Data in many schools is reported as often as six times per year! As school leaders, you need to be asking yourself these questions:

1. Is it absolutely necessary to report so frequently to parents on data that should reflect progress over time?
2. Are we actually causing more issues regarding progress, how it is measured and how we inform parents of this progress? Often teachers spend time explaining why pupils may have reached a plateau with their progress when actually they have been assessed on different skills over time and the pupils have demonstrated good progress by maintaining their level in each area. This can be time-consuming.
3. Have we placed unnecessary time constraints on our staff because of the number of times we expect data to be reported to senior leaders and parents?

I'm not suggesting that we don't measure progress because we absolutely should. There are many formative and summative ways to do so. What I am suggesting is that schools think about how they report to parents, so that they and the parents are confident that what we are reporting is a measure of progress over time, rather than an individual piece of work or a sole unit. Perhaps reporting yearly progress is the way forward? That way, parents will know how well their child has progressed over the year, and if necessary, a more comprehensive report can be shared at parents' evening.

#datadilemmas
#connect
#learn

Idea 80: New staff musts!

Taking care of new staff is crucial to building a great team.

Having worked in three different schools over my teaching career, I can tell you that starting at a new place of work is tough. However, there are policies and ideas that you can implement to make it an easier ride for any new starters. My main message to anyone responsible for new staff is this: do not assume they know everything, or even *anything*, especially if they are relatively new to teaching, but also if they are experienced members of staff. Here are just some ideas you could use.

Create a welcome pack

When I started at my most recent school, I was thrilled to be sent a welcome pack through the post. It contained everything I needed to familiarise myself with before I had even started and it felt great to feel part of the team already. By planning ahead, the school had given me time to get to know important information before I was in the thick of it. It's a great idea and was very much appreciated.

Designate a mentor

Every new staff member should have a mentor, regardless of their position. A new school is a new school. There are many things new colleagues need to know: policies, meetings, timetables and all the unwritten rules. You know the ones I mean. There's nothing worse than sitting in someone's seat in the staffroom or, worse still, using their mug. The horror! A new mentor will be useful to avoid those awkward situations.

Organise introductions

Introduce new colleagues to other staff members, especially those they are likely to come into contact with. A simple task like sending an email can be mission impossible if you don't know anyone's name. That includes support staff. Some of the most crucial colleagues in a school are the site team and the intervention staff.

Nights out

If you're new to an area, there's nothing nicer than being asked if you want to go out. You get to bond with your new colleagues and explore.

Ask new staff out or encourage their team to do so, or better still, organise a staff social and get everyone involved. You have inside information on the best places to eat, drink and be entertained. Share them! The best teams are those who show they care.

Take the time to check they're okay
It's too easy to get caught up in your own workload. Imagine you are starting a new school, with new pupils, new staff and a new area to explore. It's tough. A quick email should do the trick. I remember receiving an email simply checking if I was okay and it meant more than the sender knew on that particular day.

Allow breathing space
It takes time for new staff to settle in. Once you've given them all the information they need, let them breathe. The act of micromanaging staff is detrimental to everyone.

Smile!
Another obvious one, but so important. It's nice to feel like you belong. It can be awful if it's the opposite. Remember we're all in it for the same reason: to provide the best education we can for pupils. So smile. A friendly face can be priceless on a tough day.

Send them home early
New staff are keen to please. Avoid overloading them with extra work. Allow them time to find their feet. If you spot them working too hard, send them home early. They'll be fresher and brighter for it in the morning.

Understand
Understand that they will make mistakes. Understand it takes a lot of time to get to know pupils, and yes, they will be tested. Support them. Provide information on their pupils. Understand that policies in their previous school might have been very different. Understand that times of the day might have been different too. Understand that it's really tough to get all of this right and go home feeling like you are making a difference.

Make them feel appreciated
If they've done a good job, tell them. For new staff, positive feedback at the end of a long week is incredibly valued and makes them feel appreciated.

Everyone is equal

Regardless of their job title, make sure they are fully supported in their new role. Don't assume they know everything already. There may be data systems with which they aren't familiar, school rules that they need to learn and practices they have never before seen. Each and every school is different, so regardless of a teacher's experience, they will still need full support in a new school.

Training

If they are new to the role, make sure they have all the skills and tools they need by placing them on a valuable training course. Without the knowledge, how can you expect them to do a great job?

#newstaff
#connect
#volunteer
#learn

Idea 81: CPD sense

Ensuring staff are receiving the right training makes them feel valued and skilled.

I've lost count of the number of times I've attended whole-school CPD (continuing professional development) or CPL (continuing professional learning) over the years that has been of no use to me whatsoever. Not only that, it's also taken up precious time. Of course, school leaders have a responsibility to ensure that their staff are developed and their skills honed, yet time and time again, CPD is too generic or seen as an add-on to the school calendar. School leaders should be aware of the amount of available CPD on offer and should allow more freedom in this area if they want their staff to truly develop. It's important for teachers to realise that the learning doesn't stop after your training years. To be true 'experts' in our fields, we must continue the learning journey. Below are some suggested ways in which teachers can develop their own practice and make it specific to their needs.

- **Subject-specific training events**: These are crucial for teachers who need to develop subject knowledge in specific areas. There are many events taking place. A good place to start looking is the ResearchEd webpage, where you'll find plenty of subject-specific events: www.workingoutwhatworks.com/en-GB/Events
- **Exam board training events**: With all the new curriculum changes taking place, these are vital for lead teachers.
- **Cluster groups**: These are small groups of teachers working together on topics or subjects that matter to them. This can be across a number of schools or within a school itself. There could be a heads of department cluster group across the area, for example. Do you know what groups are available in your school's area?
- **Research groups and school working groups**: Similar to cluster groups, these groups research areas of interest and report back to their schools, implementing change as they do so. These groups are vital and in every example I have seen, they contribute much-needed knowledge and understanding in many areas of education.
- **Coaching models**: There are many types – pairs, trios and groups. They help teachers develop the skills they need to be successful and are a great way to build connections within a school.

- **TeachMeets**: I've already mentioned these in Idea 45. TeachMeets are informal gatherings where teachers come along and share ideas that have worked in their classrooms or to share reflections on teaching. They are in the style of an unconference. Teachers volunteer to present and there are always great prizes available. Staff should be encouraged to attend, as, in my experience, there is always an idea to take away and use in your classroom. You can find a list of all planned TeachMeets here: http://teachmeet.pbworks.com/w/page/19975349/FrontPage
- **NPQ Middle Leadership, Senior Leadership and Headteacher qualifications**: These are useful for teachers wishing to progress to the next stage of their career.
- **Master's degrees**: Allowing staff to complete their master's degrees is also important, as it could prove hugely beneficial in their subject field.
- **Twitter chats**: Regularly taking part in Twitter chats can also improve a teacher's knowledge. It's important that these types of events are recognised by school leaders.
- **Visiting another school**: I have often visited other schools to find out about their policies. It has resulted in some significant changes in my own school's approach.
- **Reading an educational text**: Some of my most important CPD has been reading texts about my subject. This should be considered as good CPD for staff and they should be encouraged to keep learning about their subjects.
- **Observing lessons**: Allowing staff the time to observe each other is also a great form of CPD. They can pick up a lot of ideas by simply dropping in to other teachers' lessons informally.

I think the key thing to remember here is that CPD should be tailored to each staff member. Of course, there will be times when compulsory CPD takes place, but why not allow teachers some freedom to decide what they need in order to develop? After all, it's their classroom the pupils are making progress in, so teachers are best placed to know what development needs they have to support that progress.

Next steps

Why not create a points system whereby staff have to gain a certain number of points across the year by attending different CPD events? This idea came from Jackie Smith, a science teacher and deputy head. Each event is worth a set number of points. Staff have to achieve a minimum number of points and, at the end of the year, those with the most points win prizes.

#CPDsense
#connect
#learn
#notice

Idea 82: Positive policies

Considering the workload of your staff is important for their wellbeing.

There have been times during my career where I have questioned why I have been asked to complete certain tasks. Often, it's at times when I see little impact on pupil progress but plenty of impact on my time. School leaders have a responsibility to protect the wellbeing of staff and that means ensuring policies aren't contributing unnecessarily to an already difficult workload.

School leaders should ask themselves these questions when considering policy changes and workload management.

1. Who exactly is this policy for?
Too many policies are set up to satisfy Ofsted whims and fancies or a desire for everything in schools to be measured. This takes teachers away from their actual job: to teach great lessons day in, day out.

2. What is the impact on pupil progress versus impact on teacher time?
If what you are asking your staff to do takes up too much teacher time yet has little, if any, impact on pupil progress, why on earth are you doing it?

3. What can we stop doing in order to implement this policy successfully?
Often, schools can introduce new policies and changes at the beginning of an academic year. This is fine if school leaders have considered the impact of those changes on teacher time. Teachers work flat out and at maximum capacity all year round. Before you introduce a new policy or change, something else must be taken out in order to make room for it. Far too often, I've seen staff struggle to cope with new ideas whilst still trying to maintain everything they were doing before.

Allow me to give some examples of policies I feel take up too much teacher time and have little impact on pupil progress.

Lesson plans

In some schools, mainly primary, teachers are required to write lesson plans for every lesson that they teach, every day. Of course, there is a need to demonstrate progress but there are many ways in which school leaders can monitor this that don't involve teachers spending hours scribing detailed lesson plans. Here are just a few examples:

- **PowerPoints**: Mine follow a specific structure – connect the learning, learning objectives, new information, searching for meaning, demonstrating understanding, review and reflect, and independent study. To do this and still write a lesson plan would be nonsensical.
- **Pupils' exercise books**: School leaders will be able to see whether staff have planned for learning that shows progress over time simply by looking at their pupils' exercise books. They will show clear links between lessons, topics and even separate schemes.
- **Data**: You'll be able to see which areas staff are working on based on their pupils' strengths and weaknesses. Lessons should be pitched to ensure all pupils are making progress.
- **Talk to the pupils**: They'll be able to tell you how they are moving through topics, schemes or skills. They'll be able to tell you how lessons work and what progress they are making.
- **Assessments and marking**: You'll be able to see where support is being provided based on these. Marking is part of planning.
- **Medium- and long-term plans**: These guide and direct planning.

Marking

Although the tide is turning here, there are still some schools that demand the detailed marking of every page of work. Some schools are still insisting on triple marking everything. It's madness. I'm yet to come across any research to suggest that marking has any impact on pupil progress, yet teachers up and down the country are spending hours doing it. Why? Again, to provide measures for school leaders and Ofsted.

After visiting the controversial Michaela School in London in 2016, I was impressed by their marking policy. It made perfect sense and we adapted it to fit the needs of the school I was working in at the time. Allow me to explain how it works:

- Teachers plan for progress over time. They check pupil work every two or three lessons.

- From this, they record common mistakes in learning and plan to teach the skill needed to correct the mistakes made in the previous lesson. This takes place in the same week and helps pupils make much quicker progress.
- They also record misspelled words and grammatical errors and feed these back to the pupils at the start of the next lesson. Pupils are tested at the end of the lesson on these.

So pupil work is being checked every single week. There is no delay in the feedback about how to make progress and, importantly, teacher time has been freed up dramatically so they can plan for their pupils to make even better progress.

#policyperfect
#learn
#notice

Next steps
Why not review the policies you already have in place and see if you can save staff time by making some changes? Using the questions above, you can be sure to have the pupils' learning and staff wellbeing as your focus.

Idea 83: TLR sense

Balancing responsibility across the school keeps staff wellbeing at the forefront.

Schools work much better when the responsibilities are shared out. What I mean by this is that it doesn't work to overload specific staff with too many responsibilities, as they become overworked and spread too thinly.

As school leaders, we have a responsibility to be mindful of our staff wellbeing. From a personal perspective, I know how it feels to have too many things to do and not enough time to do them. When you are working at absolute capacity, there simply isn't room for any extra responsibilities, and leaders should be mindful that their staff are naturally keen to please and may take on extra work without considering the impact on their health and wellbeing. Leaders should consider the following questions before they assign teaching and learning responsibilities (TLRs) to their colleagues:

1. Are they the right person for the job? What skills do they have that will be beneficial in the role you are seeking to fill?
2. Do they already have other responsibilities? This is important, as it can become all too easy to overload colleagues who you see as highly effective without considering the impact it could have on their wellbeing.
3. What is their timetable like? Assigning extra responsibilities to staff is great as long as you ensure they have the time to do it. If you aren't giving them any extra time, how can you be sure they will do a good job without causing some considerable impact on their wellbeing?

All too often I have seen great teachers burn out because they have taken on too much. Schools work best when responsibility is shared amongst many, not few. Leaders are responsible for ensuring their staff are not overworked, and must take an active role in protecting the wellbeing of the best assets of their school – the teachers.

#TLRsense
#notice
#connect

Idea 84: Positive perks

Small tokens of appreciation will let staff know you value them as people.

One of the big differences between the public and private sector is that the private sector seems to get quite a few more perks! But do school leaders not have a responsibility to show appreciation for staff more openly in spite of budget concerns? One of the easiest ways for school leaders to show their staff that they care is to make some simple, cheap and effective changes. Below are some ideas.

- **Free tea and coffee**: This costs very little but shows staff that they are valued and cared for. At one school I worked at, this perk was suddenly taken away at the beginning of a new academic year. There were plenty of disgruntled staff members and the leadership team soon realised they needed to reverse their decision!
- **Flu jabs**: Why not offer your staff free flu jabs over the winter term? They're great value for money to keep your team healthy and to show that you care.
- **Use of the fitness facilities**: Many schools now have fantastic resources for those wishing to keep fit. Why not offer staff free use of these facilities once the pupils have left for the day? I have some great memories of staff badminton matches.
- **Flexible working hours**: This may sound unworkable given that teachers need to be in front of their classes but there are ways around it. If a staff member takes on extra revision sessions during the holidays, for example, they could be offered a day in lieu, which they could then use for a long weekend away when they need it most. You could also offer teachers who are parents the opportunity to take paid leave for childcare reasons, as long as they manage to cover their lessons. This means they don't miss out on their own child's sports day, for example. It is gestures like this by senior leadership that show staff they are cared for. I know some schools allow staff to go home early if they don't teach during the last period. Trusting your staff to do the right thing shows support and builds community spirit. Likewise, although part-time staff can be difficult to timetable, allowing staff the freedom to choose a part-time option will certainly show you encourage flexibility at your school.

- **Encourage staff to grow as teachers and as people too**: I have been lucky enough to have been invited to present on wellbeing at teaching conferences during the working week. If it wasn't for a very understanding headteacher by the name of Tony Fitzpatrick, I wouldn't have been able to go. Luckily, he saw the importance of the event and gave me permission to attend. It's important that school leaders encourage this kind of nourishment in order for their employees to develop. We do this for our pupils, so why not extend it to staff too?
- **Plan CPD and twilight training with wellbeing in mind**: Careful planning of CPD and staff training days is another way you can ensure staff wellbeing is considered. Why not spread the training out over the year with a series of afternoon training sessions and have a day off at the end of the year? Many schools do this now and it really shows staff that you have thought about their wellbeing. This was in place at a school I worked in and not only did we accrue a day off at the end of a term, we were also allowed to leave school at midday on the last day of term. This gave the end of term a celebratory feel and, of course, instead of going home, everyone gathered together for drinks in the local watering hole. A true sign of a community-minded school.

Next steps

What else could you offer your staff to encourage retention and develop a valued community? Are there any healthcare packages at affordable rates that you could invest in? Towards the end of the summer term, why not do some research into what works best in the private sector?

#perksofateacher
#connect
#exercise
#learn
#notice

Idea 85: Awareness days

Awareness days bring school communities together whilst showing support for external causes.

A great way to bring the school community together is to hold awareness days in school. They can be linked to whole-school competitions so the entire school can get involved, even the parents! They lend themselves perfectly to whole-school wellbeing.

Below are just some of the national and international days that schools can get involved with. Exact dates can vary year to year, so check online before making plans.

January – February: Big Schools' Birdwatch

27 January: Holocaust Memorial Day

28 January – 4 February: National Storytelling Week

5 February: Safer Internet Day

17 February: Random Acts of Kindness Day

19 – 25 February: Pupil Volunteer Week

1 March: World Book Day

21 March: World Poetry Day

22 April: Earth Day

5 June: World Environment Day

9 – 17 June: Bike Week

11 – 15 June: BNF Healthy Eating Week

20 – 26 June: Recycle Now Week

11 July: World Population Day

15 July: World Youth Skills Day

8 September: International Literacy Day

13 September: Roald Dahl Day

21 September: International Day of Peace

October: Black History Month

October: International Walk to School Month

October: International School Library Month

1 October: The Big Draw

11 November: Armistice Day

12 – 16 November: National School Meals Week

10 December: Human Rights Day

The best way to have as much impact as possible with awareness days is to align them with your school's values and ethos. There's no point tagging on awareness days to tick a few school improvement boxes. They will be far more valued if you genuinely believe they are important and can add value to your pupils' wellbeing.

Next steps

Plan ahead and have these events in the school diary long before the beginning of the new academic year. Assign staff to lead on them and make sure they have enough time to do so properly.

#awarenessdays
#connect
#learn
#notice

Idea 86: Animal magic

Caring for animals benefits pupils and staff alike.

Any pet owner will tell you that animals have a significant impact on their wellbeing. However, the evidence supporting the benefits of owning a pet is not just anecdotal; there is much research to support the case too. I know schools that are real animal havens, with alpacas in the school field and visiting lambs during spring. Many schools now have school dogs too. If you aren't able to go to these lengths, why not have a small school pet – a rabbit or even some stick insects – that pupils are encouraged to care for? Below are just some of the benefits of having animals in your school.

- They reduce stress. Research in the US has proven that people who own pets are less stressed when conducting certain tasks if their pets are with them during the task.
- They improve mood. Pets really can improve a person's mood. This is one of the main reasons pets are used in different types of therapy. In some cases, dogs are used to help soldiers recover from post-traumatic stress disorder, for example.
- They improve socialisation skills. Owning pets actually improves socialisation skills, as they lead people into situations in which they will have to interact with others.
- They prevent allergies and improve immunity. Research shows that owning pets as a child actually prevents allergies later in life.
- They support emotional development. Pets help pupils develop emotionally as they learn how to express themselves and empathise. The sensory aspect of pet care also supports pupils with autism.
- They build a sense of responsibility. For pupils with attention deficit hyperactivity disorder (ADHD), for example, pet care can encourage them to be responsible through caring and an effective routine.

Next steps

Why not encourage responsibility even further by allowing pupils to take pets home over half term? You could even allow pupils the opportunity to look after the animals during break or lunch.

#animalmagic
#connect
#volunteer
#learn

Idea 87: Thank a teacher tim

Allowing pupils the opportunity to thank their teachers makes teachers feel valued.

It always amazes me how busy schools are. The amount of work that every person puts into one day of teaching is astonishing. It can be too easy to simply accept this as the norm without really thinking about it. This allows pupils to accept their teacher's efforts as a given and, at times, it can feel like they ask the world of you without any real understanding of what you do and the effort you put in. I've known pupils who have expected me to give up my lunch time to support them or, worse, demanded that I spend an hour with them after school to help them catch up. Now, of course, many teachers do offer intervention or revision sessions to their pupils out of their own goodwill, including myself. However, when pupils begin to demand such things as the norm, one could argue that things have gone slightly askew.

Allowing pupils the opportunity to thank their teachers is hugely beneficial here. The idea works like this:

- On the last Monday of every half term, hand pupils three 'thank a teacher' slips each.
- They can then thank three of their teachers for something they did for them during that half term.
- The slips are placed in a central collection point – a ballot-style box will suffice – and delivered to teachers at the end of the week.

The advantages for teacher wellbeing are clear. It encourages pupils to recognise the hard work that their teachers put in for them. This makes it less likely that they will make unreasonable demands and more likely that they will come to appreciate people for what they do, which is an all-round better outcome. Obviously, no teacher expects thanks for what they do. The pupils' progress is their reward and the reason they chose to teach in the first place, but it is always nice to feel appreciated. What better way than to receive a whole bunch of thank you notes from the pupils you support?

#thankateacher
#notice

Idea 88: Parents' evening

Parents' evenings are time-consuming for teachers and parents. Is there another way?

I think the whole process of parents' evening is poorly designed. Whoever thought that after a full day of teaching, it would be a good idea to line up endless appointments for staff well into the evening that equate to at least another half day's work? Particularly in secondary schools, parents also feel frustrated when they are forced to wait around all evening until they get a snippet of opportunity to speak to each of their child's individual teachers. Surely there is a better way to communicate with parents? I urge school leaders to reconsider evenings like this in favour of more sensible approaches.

Here are a few ideas:

Pupil review days
This idea came about at a school in Suffolk called Sudbury Upper School and Arts College. The school closes for the day and tutors meet with the parents of each of their tutees for 20 minutes. This gives them the opportunity to provide a detailed account of the pupil's progress using information gathered from subject teachers. The school were much more successful in reaching all parents in this way and attendance was high. The added benefit was that there were far fewer parents' evenings during the year.

Celebrate pupil success openly
Why not create a market stall evening where parents are encouraged to come along and look at the work pupils have produced in each subject area? Displays could be up and teachers could have pupil work available to show parents. This is a far more relaxed evening, whereby parents get to choose which areas they go to, and it creates an atmosphere of celebration. Parents could have the opportunity to discuss concerns with teachers throughout the night (pre-booked) in a separate room, but the focus would be on the success of all pupils in the main hall. The number of appointments would fall, as parents would only need to book appointments if they had concerns about their child.

Virtual parents' evenings

Why not eradicate appointments altogether in favour of a more sensible way of communicating? My school is a 'Google School', which means the opportunity to communicate with parents digitally is there. By creating this virtual forum, parents could access the information they need about their child without the necessity of travelling to school merely to spend hours waiting in queues for their turn with the next teacher. Virtual communication is becoming more popular in many schools and it supports teacher wellbeing, as it reduces the need for parents' evenings after a long day at work, as well as providing effective communication with parents.

#parentsevening
#connect
#learn
#notice

Idea 89: Staff surveys

Staff surveys enable school leaders to address wellbeing concerns.

Staff surveys should be an absolute must for any school. The most important resource in any school is the teachers themselves, and if school leaders never ask their opinion on anything or find out how they feel about certain issues, they are ignoring their most important assets.

Kerry McFarlane (@KAB21MAC) suggests that a good place to begin with this idea would be to use the HSE Management Standards (www. hse.gov.uk/stress/standards) to inform your survey. Kerry suggests adapting the following areas: demands, control, role, relationships, change and support. From this, conduct a staff wellbeing survey that will give you a baseline to identify and evaluate issues. Kerry also suggests creating an online anonymous survey to encourage honest responses and a greater uptake in completed surveys. She also commented that it is important that staff feel supported every day and that school leaders must be committed to developing a climate of support amongst staff. Staff must feel that the exercise is genuine, rather than a tick-box, tokenistic activity.

Once the survey has been completed, a number of actions could be introduced according to the needs of the staff in your school. Some ideas could include: introducing #teacher5aday via staff meetings; introducing a coaching model that fits the bespoke needs of your staff; workload initiatives to reduce time spent planning and marking; and a whole host of other ideas. You could even introduce some of the ideas in this book (ahem!).

> **Next steps**
> Once the initial survey is complete and you have actioned a number of ideas as a result of the survey, it would be a good idea (as suggested by Kerry) to do a follow-up survey and identify next steps. Wellbeing is a priority for all school leaders and should remain one consistently in education.

#staffsurvey
#connect
#notice

Idea 90: Leadership logic

Promoting leadership in schools develops the whole school community.

School leaders have an important role when it comes to appointing new leaders. There can often be a misconception that if a person is an outstanding teacher, they will automatically make a great leader. That is not always the case. Excellent exam results and successful teaching don't necessarily mean someone is a great leader. When deciding on which staff members would make good leaders for the school, current school leaders should ask themselves the following questions:

1. Has the candidate shown the necessary leadership skills required to undertake the role? Or do they have the capacity to develop them quickly?
2. Has the candidate shown the necessary management skills required to undertake the role? Or do they have the capacity to develop them quickly?
3. Do the candidate's vision and ethos align with those of the school? This is important, as they will be representing the school's views.
4. Does the candidate have good relationships with colleagues in school? They will need excellent interpersonal skills to take up the position.

These are just a few starting questions to consider. Essentially, the interviewers will have to decide if the candidate is a good fit for their school, and that will be down to each individual candidate to prove.

Once in a role, it's important that schools support their leaders to do a great job. Some leaders may need more support than others. To that end, it's always a good idea to offer some training and support to school leaders. There are many courses available but it would again be down to each individual leader as to what needs they have. Taking on a leadership role in a school can be quite a daunting experience for some teachers. It can suddenly feel quite a lonely place to be, as you are no longer 'one of the gang'. It's the school's responsibility to ensure they feel fully supported, so they can perform well and feel successful.

#leadershiplogic
#notice

Index